ALSO BY MICHAEL E. ADDIS, PH.D.

*Depression in Context*
(with Christopher Martell and Neil Jacobson)

*Ending Depression One Step at a Time*
(with Christopher Martell)

# INVISIBLE MEN

# Invisible Men

## MEN'S INNER LIVES AND THE CONSEQUENCES OF SILENCE

**MICHAEL E. ADDIS, PH.D.**

TIMES BOOKS   HENRY HOLT AND COMPANY   NEW YORK

Times Books
Henry Holt and Company, LLC
*Publishers since 1866*
175 Fifth Avenue
New York, New York 10010

Henry Holt® is a registered trademark of Henry Holt and Company, LLC.

Library of Congress Cataloging-in-Publication Data

Addis, Michael E.
    Invisible men : men's inner lives and the consequences of silence / Michael E. Addis.—1st ed.
        p.    cm.
    Includes bibliographical references and index.
    ISBN 978-0-8050-9200-4 (hardcover)
    1. Masculinity.    I. Title.
    BF692.5.A337    2011
    155.3'32—dc22                                                                2011001184

Henry Holt books are available for special promotions and
premiums. For details contact: Director, Special Markets.

First Edition 2011

*Designed by Kelly S. Too*

Printed in the United States of America

1    3    5    7    9    10    8    6    4    2

For Barnett Roy Addis

1932–2009

# CONTENTS

# PREFACE

When I began this book one thing was very clear. I knew that I wanted to write about silence, invisibility, and all the other things that make it so difficult for us to truly see and hear men's vulnerability. On the other hand, one thing was not clear to me at all: a title. *Silent Pain?* Too touchy-feely. *The Role of Hidden Vulnerability in Men's Lives?* Yawn. Way too academic. Then about a week into writing I found myself organizing some old books in my office. Anyone who writes regularly will tell you that organizing is a great way to avoid putting fingers to keyboard. Still, it was my organizing that led me to a collection of novels I had gathered beginning in high school and on through college and graduate school. Among them were H. G. Wells's *The Invisible Man* and Ralph Ellison's *Invisible Man*. "Hmm," I thought to myself, "books about invisible men. I seem to be writing one too."

And that's when my struggle started. I certainly did not want to be accused of placing myself in the company of such great writers as Wells and Ellison. And particularly in the case of Ellison, as a white male academic I was easily open to the criticism of co-opting Ellison's creative metaphor for race relations and repackaging it from a generic and privileged "raceless" perspective; not a good thing for a social scientist. Plus, let's be honest—like most people, I prefer to be liked.

For several weeks I shied away from anything with the word *invisible* in it. But nothing captured both the immediacy and the scope of the issues like *Invisible Men*. Plus, I was finding that my own struggle with the title was beginning to shed some light on another aspect of invisibility in men's lives, one I had never considered. The thrust of this book is the notion that, when it comes to their own human vulnerability, silence and invisibility are perennial and powerful issues in men's lives. That idea was familiar to me. What I was less familiar with is the notion that men, not as nongendered, universal, human beings, but "as men," have been remarkably invisible in many books that contain the words *man* or *men* in the title. In other words, the problem is not only that men's vulnerability is often invisible. It's also that men themselves, as men, are often invisible.

Take Wells's and Ellison's books. *The Invisible Man*, so we are told, is a science fiction novel about technology and its effects on human relationships and communities. Ellison's *Invisible Man* is typically presented as a narrative about the wide range of race-related issues facing African Americans in the early to mid-twentieth century. There are contemporary examples as well. When I teach courses on the psychology of men, I assign *A Man in Full* by Tom Wolfe, a novel that was published shortly before 9/11 and one that I interpret as largely about the breakdown of traditional masculinity along social, economic, and relational lines. However, a quick Internet search of the book's title, along with the terms *masculinity* and *gender*, reveals virtually no commentary suggesting that this might actually be a book about men, per se. And then there is the classic film *Fight Club*, a powerfully disturbing story of one man's attempt to create a meaningful sense of self through brutal combat with other men. Early in the film we learn about the first rule of fight club: don't talk about fight club. In other words, keep it silent and invisible.

I began to realize that even though men and invisibility have shared titles at various points in the last century, the actual issue of men's invisibility has been, well, invisible. The more I thought about it, the more convinced I became that the title *Invisible Men* makes perfect sense. This book is about nothing more, and nothing less, than the widespread silence and invisibility that affect all men's lives, and the price we all pay for it.

*Invisible Men* is full of stories and anecdotes about men's lives. When referring to friends, family members, or acquaintances I either omit their names or provide pseudonyms. In each case individuals provided consent to have their stories told. Some anecdotes come from situations I observed while living life outside my role as a research psychologist (playing golf, for example). In these instances I changed many of the identifying characteristics of individuals and created pseudonyms to protect anonymity. The remaining sources come either from research interviews conducted at Clark University or from former clients to whom I provided counseling. Pseudonyms are provided for each of these cases, and identifying characteristics were changed. Some of these are composites of a few different individuals developed for the purpose of illustrating a particular point.

# INVISIBLE MEN

# PART I

---

# THE PROBLEM:
# SILENCE, INVISIBILITY, AND
# MEN'S VULNERABILITY

# Prologue

*Patrick's Story*

Several years ago I was working in an inpatient psychiatric unit in the Pacific Northwest. As a psychology intern, my job was to come in early, read through the charts of the patients admitted the previous evening, and be prepared to do their intake interviews by 8:00 a.m. After six years of doctoral training, this was my first exposure to persistent and severe human suffering of the type that frequently turns into a crisis.

Often, patients were admitted because they had attempted to harm themselves, or they were at risk of harming themselves, or they had begun to lose touch with reality in a variety of ways. As tragic as each of these individual cases was, there were certain similarities that kept returning as I read about more and more of them. In many of the cases the patient was a woman. There was often overt relationship conflict involved, either with a significant other or with family members. Frequently there was a fairly lengthy history of psychiatric treatment in the patient's file. Patients were also often strapped for resources and living at or below the poverty line.

One morning, in midwinter, I picked up a chart that struck

me as quite different from the very first page. Patrick was a white, middle-aged, married man with no history of previous psychiatric illness. His chart contained only a brief description of the events that preceded his admission to the hospital. Apparently, Patrick's wife was out for the evening, and his teenage son was supposed to be spending the night at a friend's house. However, following a change of plans, Patrick's son returned earlier than expected and discovered his father sitting on the couch with a loaded shotgun pointed at his head. His son called 911, the police came, and Patrick was taken to the ER. When asked what he was intending to do with the shotgun, Patrick replied simply, "End it." In response to my question asking why he wanted to take his own life, he stated only "Enough is enough" and refused to elaborate.

That morning I interviewed Patrick one-on-one. When he walked into the room I immediately knew that it was going to be difficult to connect with him and to find out what was really going on. Although he was dressed in hospital clothes and apparently had neither shaven nor combed his hair for several days, I could immediately see that Patrick was (or had been) a handsome man who surely stood out in a crowd. His short salt-and-pepper hair, dark green eyes, tanned skin, and muscular physique made an impression even in his current condition. Patrick looked like someone who could have been a football coach, a banker, a politician, or a mountain climber. Yet now he was clearly half of a person; someone whose former life was a distant and painful memory, and someone whose current life wasn't particularly worth living.

Patrick looked down at his lap during the initial part of the interview. He answered my questions in a courteous fashion, but his tone was matter-of-fact and he did not elaborate on any of his answers. He identified no reason for wanting to take his life other than what he had stated previously ("Enough is enough"). All of my attempts to empathize with Patrick seemed to clam him up even more. I began to wonder if a sense of having failed in some way had played a role in leading Patrick to consider suicide.

Eventually, and partly out of frustration, I leaned forward in my chair with my elbows on my knees. "Patrick, I've got to tell you, I can't understand what got you to this point. None of this really seems to add up," I said. "Can we be straight with each other and cut out the BS?"

Patrick began to tell me about the events of his life over the previous two years. He had been running a very successful self-made company. Through hard work and a series of calculated investment risks, Patrick had built the business to a point where he was able to move his family into a larger house with a lakefront view. His family and friends were aware of Patrick's successes, which were a source of substantial pride on his part. People knew him as an easygoing guy with a good sense of humor who was, in many ways, a model of successful manhood as it has been traditionally defined.

Then a series of setbacks occurred. First, a major consulting job did not pan out. Then one of his previous clients developed financial difficulties and began spreading the word that it was Patrick's fault. Patrick's own business steadily slowed until he had difficulty making a mortgage payment on the new house. Things went downhill financially from there. Then the economy crashed. It was Patrick's response to these events that really struck me. Rather than letting his wife and close friends know about the struggles he was facing, Patrick kept it all to himself. Over time, the gap between what people *thought* was going on in his life and what was *actually* going on grew larger, and Patrick became profoundly depressed. He couldn't face working, but he also couldn't face telling people how bad things had gotten. Instead, he got up each morning, dressed as if he was going to work, forced a smile for his family, and either drove around the city or sat at a local coffee shop all day reading the newspaper. Eventually the depression became so overwhelming that he saw no other way out.

"How could I face them?" he asked. "What would they think of me? In their eyes I'd look like a has-been, somebody whose time had come and gone, only because he couldn't handle it."

"But those were extremely difficult experiences you had," I said. "Nobody could have foreseen the financial difficulties."

"I should have been able to. Besides, that's not what I'm talking about. I should have been able to handle it emotionally. Instead, I fell apart and turned into a sniveling little boy. What was I going to say, 'Oh, Mommy, please help me?' I couldn't let people see me like that."

On the one hand, it seemed obvious to me that no man would want to see himself like a little boy asking for Mommy's help. But then if you stopped and thought about it, is asking for help worse than dying? How far will a man go to hide his shame? How many Patricks are there who would rather take their own lives than try to break through the gauntlet of silence and invisibility that prevents them from finding the support they so desperately need?

# 1

# Invisible Men . . .
# Who Are You Kidding?!

The title of this book may make you wonder, "Invisible men . . . who are you kidding?" Everywhere we look we see men's lives. On television, in sports, in politics, at work, and at home, men are anything but invisible. At the same time, most men's inner lives remain hidden from others and often from themselves. For centuries, men have been taught that their uncertainty, their pain, and their fear are not for public consumption; how a man really feels about his marriage, his job, his child's sickness, or himself should be kept extremely close to the vest, except under the most unusual circumstances. The bottom line is that a man's masculinity is measured in large part by his ability to make his public accomplishments widely *seen* and *heard*, while keeping his inner life *silent* and *invisible*.

This book is about the wide range of problems created by the silence and invisibility that often surround men's inner lives. These problems affect not only men but also women, children, communities, and our increasingly global society. To some degree, the feminist revolution of the 1960s and '70s raised our awareness of the damaging effects of traditional masculine roles. Yet despite this awareness, very little has changed; when emotions are running high, many men still leave the house, go on long walks, or head to the nearest bar; wives still implore men to talk about their feelings, only to be told "not now," "later," and "this is not the time."

The expectation remains that men should not get sad. They should get angry, watch sports, or drink, but they should not share their feelings. Research shows that many men who experience depression and anxiety have tremendous difficulty seeking help. For most men, admitting that they are suffering internally is more difficult than admitting that they are an alcoholic or a drug addict. After all, it is more socially acceptable for a man to be a "drunk" or a "grouch" than to suffer from what society deems a "women's issue." Thus their inner lives remain silent.

For this, men pay heavily. Recent studies have shown that conforming to traditional gender roles predicts aspects of men's functioning as diverse as a decreased sense of well-being following prostate cancer surgery, lower levels of health-promoting behaviors, higher levels of health risk behaviors, and higher levels of drug and alcohol abuse. Men still die five to seven years younger than women, and they far surpass women in rates of substance abuse, anger, aggression, and violent crime. Recent estimates suggest that 6 to 8 percent of men will suffer an episode of major depression in a given year, and 13 to 19 percent will experience a major anxiety attack. Although women are twice as likely as men to attempt suicide, men are *four times as likely* as women to actually take their own lives.[1-3] It is quite likely that these problems will grow worse in the coming years unless something is done to break the shroud of silence that surrounds men's vulnerability and pain.

## ENTERING THE TERRITORY

I have spent the last ten years researching, writing, and talking to men about the problems in their lives. All of this work has convinced me of two things. First, men have a lot going on underneath the surface. Second, under the right conditions almost all men are interested in sharing what they are experiencing. This happens much more easily when both men and women understand how the silence and invisibility that surround men's inner lives operate.

Once you begin to open your eyes you can see the pain in men's lives everywhere you look. Sometimes it exists on a grand scale. Witness, for example, the increasing rates of suicide among returning veterans from the Gulf wars.[4–5] Other times, it occurs more locally, and the veil over men's pain is considerably more subtle. The following story illustrates just how common it has become to ignore the realities of men's lives.

### "CAN'T COMPLAIN"

I recently stopped by the local coffee shop near our university and ran into one of the staff members. I knew him reasonably well. We'd exchanged greetings and had brief conversations about the Red Sox every so often for over ten years. On this particular day our conversation went like this:

"How's it going?" he asks.

"Fine," I say. "How about you?"

"Can't complain," he says. "Work is work. You know?"

Then he grinned with that familiar mixture of 70 percent suppressed anger, 20 percent irony, and 10 percent real visible pain.

Of course, being a psychologist, and being interested in men's well-being, I tune in to the anger and the pain immediately. But being a man, I know my options for how to respond are very limited. I certainly am not supposed to acknowledge his inner pain directly. I am not going to say something like "You seem really stressed; how are you doing?" We simply do not go there. So instead our interaction goes this way:

"Yep. I hear you," I say. "Friday can't come soon enough."

"Oh, yeah," he replies. "I'll be heading out on my boat and knocking back a few."

I say, "Sounds good to me. Have a great weekend."

"Yep. You too," he says.

On one level, this seems like a pretty normal casual conversation between two men. And you may be asking yourself why I am making such a big deal out of it. After all, you are not going to dump an enormous load of personal information on another guy whenever he says, "How's it going?" especially in a coffee shop. Plus, guys do not talk about that stuff. Everyone knows that; it is one of the great gender truths.

But here's the thing. Although I do not know this guy well, I know him well enough to know that he has two young kids in school, one of whom has a severe learning disability. I know that he struggles financially and that the boat is probably an excess he really can't afford. I can tell from the way he walks that he has back trouble that must cause him chronic pain in his line of work. I know all of this because over time I have paid attention to subtle cues, and I have asked the periodic personal question. I know that when he says "I am fine," that's a way of saying "I have not lost it. I am still competent. I am holding it together." And when he says "I can't complain," that's a way of saying "What am I going to do about the pain in my life? You take what life gives you."

Here's what I think is going on. Millions of men are silently struggling on the inside, and they *do not have a way of talking about it.* Millions of men and women are aware that something may be wrong with the men they know and care about, but they *do not know how to talk with men about it.* As a result, we've all tacitly agreed that "Doing fine. Can't complain" is one of the few appropriate responses to the question "How's it going?"

## THE FUNDAMENTAL QUESTION

How can men, as a group, be so audible, so visible, and in such positions of power in society, and yet, as individuals, feel so disempowered and experience vulnerability and inner pain that remain silent and invisible?

This book is concerned with answering that fundamental question. The more you can understand about the causes of men's hidden suffering, the more you will be empowered to do something about it. The time has clearly come to take action. The first step is actually seeing and hearing the pain that so many men keep silent and invisible.

## FRAGILE VERSUS BRITTLE

In 1988 I went to graduate school at the University of Washington to work with Marsha Linehan, Ph.D. At that time Marsha was one of the very few clinical researchers in the world studying the causes and treatment of Borderline Personality Disorder (BPD). BPD is a severe disorder that affects a person's mood, his or her relationships with others, self-esteem, and many other parts of life. Marsha has theorized that the core problem in BPD is difficulty in regulating emotions and that many of the additional problems (e.g., frequent attempts at suicide or other forms of self-injury) are attempts to cope with emotions that are experienced as more severe and out of control.

Over the years I became more and more interested in the psychology of men, and Marsha and I lost touch. However, a few years ago our paths crossed again. Apparently Marsha had begun working with people who met criteria for BPD and were also chronic drug or alcohol abusers. It turns out that a greater percentage of these people are men (compared to those who have BPD but do not abuse drugs and alcohol). Marsha got in touch because she had heard about my work in the psychology of men. We got to talking, and I ended up inviting Marsha to give a lecture to a recently formed special interest group from the Association for Behavioral and Cognitive Therapies (ABCT.org) on men's mental and physical health. Marsha said she would be happy to give a lecture, but she was concerned that she really did not know that much about the psychology of men. "That's OK," I reassured her, "just be yourself, and it will be great." I was confident of this because Marsha is known as an incredibly creative thinker with a tremendous amount of natural intuition about human suffering.

Marsha came to the meeting and spoke to a packed audience about her experiences working with men. During the question-and-answer part of her lecture, one audience member asked, "If you had to say one thing about the difference between men and women with BPD, what would it be?" Like all good scientists, Marsha was reluctant to generalize too much without sufficient data to back her up. But she eventually succumbed to the pressure to identify a difference between men and women, and she said: "In my experience, women with BPD come across as very *fragile*. There's something about them that seems like they are barely holding it together beneath the surface and they really need my help. The men seem less fragile and more *brittle*. I am not sure what that difference is exactly. But with the men it seems like if you reach out and touch them (metaphorically speaking) they might just crack entirely."

I have thought about Marsha's statements several times since then. I have often wondered about the difference between *fragile* and *brittle* and what it may have to do with the silence and invisibility of men's inner lives. I actually think that Marsha's generalization now applies not only to people with BPD but to many women and men who are struggling with painful emotions in their lives. When I think of something being fragile, I think of needing to handle it with care. I also think of it breaking easily, but also being able to be repaired or put back together. When I think of something or someone being brittle, I think of strength and resistance up to the point of cracking, and then total disrepair. I'm not saying that men can't be helped when they have problems, or that they will inevitably "crack" if we reach out to them. What I am saying is that men's vulnerability often seems more "brittle" to themselves than it does "fragile." And if you thought that you might literally crack if you let go of your efforts to hold yourself together, wouldn't you keep things quiet and hidden?

It is important to understand that for many men the fear is not necessarily of cracking and going "insane." As one participant in our research said to me, "I do not know if I am that worried about going nuts. I mean, if I was really nuts, I probably wouldn't even know it! But it is the idea of not being able to hold it together that I can't stomach." At first I didn't understand what he was saying. But I slowly realized that he was making a very important distinction: for many men the idea that they would not be able to hold themselves together, to be in control of their minds and their emotions, is scarier and more potentially shameful than actually "going crazy." Most women know that "breaking down" and sobbing for a while does not mean you are crazy; it simply means that you are unleashing a lot of emotions. Yet for many men, keeping their true inner lives silent and invisible is not a game or really even a choice. It is a highly ingrained way of life; a survival strategy learned early on that has helped them to avoid the torrent of shame that often rains down on young boys (and men) when they let their vulnerable sides show.

## COLLATERAL DAMAGE

It is not just men who are harmed by their own silence and invisibility. Children and families can also be negatively affected. When men keep excessively quiet about their lives they are more likely to grow distant from those who love them. As many readers are undoubtedly aware, it is hard to feel close to someone who keeps everything bottled up inside. Children need to feel close to their parents. Silent and invisible men are not only affecting the quality of their relationships with their children, but also teaching those children, particularly young boys, how to handle problems in life. This is one of the major ways that the cycle is passed down from generation to generation. Work productivity can also be hindered by men's tendency to keep their real lives hidden from others. It certainly makes sense not to blurt out all your personal problems at the workplace. However, when excessive silence leads to increased depression and anxiety (as it often can), productivity decreases. In short, when men remain emotionally stoic and withdrawn, everyone suffers. Have you or someone close to you exhibited any of the following patterns of behavior?

- A man suffers the loss of a loved one and never grieves. Over the years he slowly becomes more withdrawn, has difficulty sleeping, and doesn't enjoy things as much as he used to.
- A man loses his job unexpectedly and becomes increasingly angry and bitter about life. Although he works hard to find another job, at home he seems less and less satisfied with life. His consumption of alcohol increases, and his wife and children worry more and more about him.
- A teenage boy begins to experiment with drugs and alcohol. He spends more and more time alone in his room or out late at night with friends. His grades suffer, and his parents worry about him every day. Despite their attempts to talk with him about it, he insists that nothing is wrong and nothing has changed.
- As the stress levels increase at work or school a man develops several debilitating physical symptoms such as recurrent headaches, backaches, or stomach pains. He angrily rejects the notion that he might benefit from counseling. Instead, he insists that he is not depressed, that it is "just stress," and he copes by drinking more alcohol than usual.

## SILENCE, INVISIBILITY, AND THEIR SYNONYMS

It is important to understand that silence and invisibility do not always appear in literal form. In other words, men do not always physically keep quiet or hide their feelings from others. I use the terms *silence* and *invisibility* metaphorically to describe a wide range of ways in which men's inner lives are hidden, obscured, or otherwise inaccessible to individual men or those around them. *Silence* and *invisibility* are simply shorthand ways to describe a whole list of different ways in which men's true inner lives are hidden from view. To get a sense of what I am talking about, see the accompanying box, which provides a list of synonyms for *silence* and *invisibility*.

> Shut up, hushed, shushed, hidden, unseen, undetectable, muted, noiseless, restrained, tongue-tied, unheard, zipped, concealed, covert, disguised, ghostly, masked, obscured, veiled, screened, shielded, shrouded, clandestine, off the record, cloaked, covered, clouded, cryptic, in the dark, screened, shadowy, underground, stealthy, under wraps, cloak and dagger, furtive, camouflaged

It is also important to understand the difference between what behaviors look like and how they function. The same behavior can have different consequences depending on when and how it occurs. Literally not talking about problems in your life can be a way to avoid painful feelings and may promote depression or other mental health issues. Alternatively, not talking can promote intimacy, as when couples sit quietly together and communicate by sharing an experience without necessarily talking. One of the goals of this book is to help you recognize when silence is a problem and when it is not. Doing so requires you to raise your awareness of the many different ways that silence and invisibility can operate in a man's life. This is easier to do when you understand what it feels like.

## THE THREE P'S OF SILENCE

### PERSONAL SILENCE

Men's silence can occur in at least three different ways. The first is *personal silence*. This is the sort of silence that occurs when a man himself does not even know that he is in pain. It has been suggested that most men are raised in such a way that they develop a mild version of a psychological condition known as *alexithymia*.[6–7] The term literally translates as "without words for mood." In other words, on average, men may have difficulty putting what they are feeling into words.

You may wonder what it feels like to experience personal silence on a regular basis. In the book *Masculinity Reconstructed*,[8] the psychologist Ronald Levant and coauthor Gini Kopecky tell the story of a man whose son canceled a father-son outing to a hockey game. The man had been looking forward to the outing and was obviously distressed when relaying the series of events to Levant. Levant asked the man how he felt when his son canceled, but the man couldn't answer the question. All he could say was, "He shouldn't have done it." This man was *entirely unable to describe what he felt internally*. It was only after Levant showed the man a videotape of himself describing the situation that the man was able to *logically infer* that he must have felt disappointed. This is a classic example of personal silence; a man's inner life is so silent that even he can't hear it.

You might be thinking that ignorance is bliss. After all, if you do not even know that you are feeling something painful, how painful could it actually be? Maybe those people who are often personally silent are actually happier than those who tend to know what they are feeling. Unfortunately, it doesn't usually work that way. Clinical psychologists have long noted that people who tend to be largely unaware of what they are feeling still express it in other ways, many of which can be equally or more troubling than the original feelings themselves. Unexplained medical conditions, for example, can often emerge in response to significant life stress. At a very basic immunological level it is clear that too much stress puts us at risk for a wide range of health problems. All of this is at least workable if we know when we are stressed. We can put the stress into words, perhaps share it with others, and do things to mitigate the effects of it. But what if you don't even know when you are unhappy? What do you do then?

I once worked with a man named Doug who had gotten divorced, lost his job, and moved away from his children all within the span of one year. Doug was referred to me by his primary care physician, whom he saw initially because of headaches, back pain, and difficulty sleeping. His PCP did the right thing by running some basic tests, and also inquiring about potential stress-ors in Doug's life. As you might expect, the medical tests revealed nothing wrong, so the PCP suggested that Doug might benefit from talking with a psychologist about some of the stresses he was facing.

When I met with him I acknowledged that Doug had been through quite a bit in a short period of time and asked him how he felt about it all. Our conversation went something like this:

ME: How do you feel about all of this?

DOUG: I don't know. Bad, I guess.

ME: Do you feel depressed at times?

DOUG: I don't think so.

ME: How about anxious?

DOUG: I don't know. I am not sure what that feels like.

ME: When you are sitting at home thinking about your kids, the divorce, and other things, how does your body feel? What do you notice about it?

DOUG: I'm not sure. Sort of tense, I guess.

ME: Do you think the stress you are experiencing could be creating the physical problems?

DOUG: I don't know. Isn't that what you're supposed to figure out?


I worked with Doug for several months, and over time he began to be better able to identify the emotions he was experiencing, including guilt, sadness, and fear about the future. Working with him was not so much a matter of "therapy" in the traditional sense of uncovering childhood traumas, analyzing dreams, and so on. It was more about simply teaching him a vocabulary to identify and express what he was experiencing privately. Given that his life had just been turned on its head, he had a lot going on.

As Doug's ability to verbalize his emotional experience increased, his physical symptoms decreased. He was also better able to communicate with his children, and to share with them his feelings about the recent life changes that affected all of them.

I think about his story whenever I am reminded of the tremendous value that emotions offer to human beings; they are powerful messengers that tell us about our relationship to our environment at any point in time. If things are going well, we tend to feel good. If not, we tend to feel bad. But if we can't know what we are feeling because of excessive personal silence, it can be very hard to know what to do when we are not quite getting along with the world, so to speak.

## PRIVATE SILENCE

If personal silence is about not knowing what is going on inside of you, private silence is about knowing what is going on but choosing to keep it private. Private silence is of course very useful and appropriate under the right circumstances. We all know people who tend to keep things to themselves; it's a common character trait in both men and women. On the other hand, private silence can become a problem when it is not a choice but a default setting that rarely if ever changes.

### Mike's Story

Mike was a sixty-two-year-old working-class man who responded to a newspaper ad our research group had placed. We were looking for men who were experiencing so much stress that it got in the way of their lives, and also men who preferred to handle problems on their own. Mike arrived at our interview dressed in denim shorts, a baggy T-shirt, and a John Deere baseball cap. When I asked what led him to respond to the advertisement, Mike took a deep breath and then told me the story of his daughter, who had recently returned home after serving three years in the military in Iraq. Mike took great joy and pride in their relationship. They were extremely close and talked openly about their love for each other.

However, after returning home, Mike's daughter spent the majority of her time in bed and watching television. Eventually she became so withdrawn and depressed that she stopped speaking. Mike could not understand what was happening, but he felt his daughter's pain acutely. "It was like watching a part of myself fade away, and knowing there was nothing I could do to stop it," he told me. When he said this, I thought of my own daughter and what it would be like to lose her; a thought that was too terrifying to entertain for more than a second.

If that weren't enough, what Mike told me next made me want to flee the room. One morning Mike went to check on his daughter and found her dead in bed. Her heart had stopped beating for no apparent reason. I asked Mike how he had been coping with such a traumatic experience. He only said, "I try to go on. Try to remember what a good person she was." I then asked Mike if he talked with his wife about their daughter's death. He said that the subject was too painful to discuss. When I asked if there was anyone else he had shared this with, he said, "Nope. No one, at least until now." I asked Mike what it was like to talk about it, and he began to cry. "It's OK," he said. "Kind of good actually to get it off my chest."

Part of my research with my colleagues involves developing ways to help motivate men to share their struggles with others and to ask for help when necessary. Mike and I began to discuss the pros and cons of talking to more people about what happened with his daughter. Some of the pros included getting things off his chest, being able to share positive feelings about her with others, bringing some closure to the situation, and simply being around others as opposed to being isolated. Some of the cons included having to experience painful emotions and facing the possibility that others wouldn't be supportive. As we talked more, it became clear to Mike that the potential pros far outweighed the cons. Still, I did not push him in any particular direction, and he made no specific plans.

When we met one week later, I asked Mike if anything stood out about our interview the previous week. Mike again mentioned that it was good to get things off his chest, and then he told me that he had called his doctor to see whether some medication might help with the depression he was experiencing. He also called a close friend of his and asked if they could get together and talk. When Mike told his friend about his daughter's death, the friend hugged him and asked him why he hadn't brought up the subject sooner. He also told Mike that he would always be there for him if he wanted to talk.

Mike found the interaction with his friend to be an enormous relief. He told me that it was difficult to make the call because he did not feel like he was justified in asking for his friend's help; in Mike's mind his problems were not bad enough to warrant reaching out to others. But what Mike was able to do was to respond differently to his own inner life, dark and troubled as it was. Rather than continuing to keep things private, he shared them with someone close to him. And rather than assume that he alone was responsible for coping with the pain he was feeling, he took the chance to seek help from someone else.

When I asked Mike how he was able to make such a dramatic change, his response said it all: "Sixty-two years of this stuff is enough. Enough of the tough-it-out, go-it-alone, soldier-on stuff. It never really worked for my father and it wasn't really working for me, so I decided to try something different."

Mike's story highlights several pathways to change that I will explore in part 2. First, old dogs can learn new tricks. It is never too late for men to change, and in fact research has shown that as men approach retirement age they often become more interested in family relationships and in developing connections with others. At the same time, rates of depression increase as men age. As a society, and as individuals, we must reach out to older men and let them know that we are interested in their lives.

Second, men must be supported in coping with grief. Divorce, loss of a child, loss of friends and family members, and even loss of a job are powerful experiences for all human beings. Unfortunately, as a culture we have not been tolerant and supportive of men in grieving these losses. Friends and family members need to ask how men are doing and not be deterred by an initial, "fine" response. Men can hear and feel love and support from others, even if we can't always express it. A simple "I've been thinking about you; let me know if you ever want to talk" can send a very powerful message to a man that his inner life is no longer off-limits. It is then his choice whether he wants to share it with others.

Third, major societal and cultural events can have a powerful effect on our openness to seeing and hearing men's inner lives. Were it not for the war in Iraq, Mike's daughter would probably not have been in the military, and thus would not have developed the severe case of post-traumatic stress disorder that went unrecognized, untreated, and ultimately led to her death. As veterans return home, suicide rates are dramatically increasing; recent estimates suggest that one veteran from the Iraq war is committing suicide every five days. As a result, we are seeing more openness in the media to recognizing that men do indeed suffer from traumatic stress, and that something needs to be done about it. Similarly, in the weeks directly following 9/11, we saw policemen and firefighters shedding tears over the emotional devastation they were experiencing. These images and stories help to *normalize* men's pain. The more we see it, the less shocking and stigmatizing it becomes.

As it turns out, excessive private silence can create substantial problems for people. And, not surprisingly, it tends to be more common in men. Research has shown that men are much less likely than women to discuss problems with others.[9–11] This includes not only friends and acquaintances, but also family members and other loved ones. In addition, it is well established that having others close at hand to confide in is associated with positive health benefits, both physical and mental. In other words, people who are excessively private tend to have fewer people in their networks of support, and therefore fewer people to turn to in times of trouble. These same people tend to be at greater risk for mental and physical health problems as a result. Let me be clear here. I am not saying that sharing *everything* in your life with *everyone* in your life is healthy. What I am saying is that excessive privacy is just as unhealthy as excessive "dumping" on others.

## PUBLIC SILENCE

Before they reach adolescence, young boys are often remarkably free of excessive personal or private silence. They share their fears and worries with parents, express loving tender feelings toward friends and family, and are capable of having a very rich emotional vocabulary. At the same time, knowing that adolescence is just around the corner, the parents of a young boy may already begin to mourn for the potential (and perhaps likely) loss of their son's honesty and sensitivity.

Adolescence is a time characterized, among other things, by huge waves of public silencing in boys' lives. Public silence occurs when people in your environment let you know, in one way or another, that they do not want to hear about your vulnerability. This can happen in ways that range from subtle (changing the topic) to flat out in your face ("Dude, I don't know what you're whining about, everybody's got problems. Suck it up and move on"). It's not hard to imagine how the experience of public silencing can lead to greater levels of personal and private silence. Many of the men I have spoken with in our research describe early painful and often traumatic experiences with public silencing. As a result, some have chosen to remain privately silent in order to avoid similar shameful and humiliating experiences in the future. For others it is not really a choice. They have simply stopped paying attention to what is going on inside of them and are personally silent as well.

Public silencing is not limited to adolescence. In fact, it is alive and well in the lives of many adult men who might otherwise risk exposing their need for support during difficult times in their lives.

### Sal's Story

Several years ago I headed down to the local nine-hole golf course on a beautiful sunny fall day hoping to join up as a single player with some others for an afternoon of relaxation and fun (as much as golf can be relaxing!). I was fortunate to meet up with three other men, none of whom I had played with previously. Each of them appeared to be well past the usual retirement age, and I had the sense that they had known each other for a very long time.

As it turned out, I was right. They ribbed each other after poor tee shots and missed putts, congratulated each other when things went well, and recalled many shared golfing adventures together. I found them to be an enjoyable group and was relieved when they began to welcome me by making fun of my inevitable blunders on the course. (I have since quit playing golf after recognizing that one need not spend large sums of money to become frustrated and self-critical for several hours. But that's another story . . . )

The fourth hole was a long par three over water, and we waited on the tee while the group ahead of us finished. Because we were not directly involved in playing golf at that moment there was an opportunity for a bit more sustained conversation. At one point, Fred turned to Sal and started the following dialogue:

FRED: So what is new in your neck of the woods, Sal?

SAL: Well, shit. Nothing you wouldn't expect, except maybe I had a prostate biopsy last week.

FRED: Oh yeah [*laughing*], was it good for you?

SAL: What? What the fuck are you talking about?

FRED: You know [*turning to the rest of us*], they've got to get up there somehow. At least that's what they tell me. But not me. I won't even let my doctor put on a rubber glove [*laughs*].

SAL: You guys are sick. You think I like this?

FRED: I don't know, what do you think, guys? I've wondered about Sal, haven't you?

SAL: Like I said, you guys are sick.

Where to start? First, it is remarkable how quickly Sal's vulnerability was shut down by Fred's response to Sal's disclosure that he had had a prostate biopsy. Fred's jokes made it very clear to everyone involved, and especially to Sal, that this was not to be treated as a serious topic. Second, the transparently homophobic nature of Fred's comments served to shame Sal for even bringing the topic up. As we will see in chapter 2, boys and men use homophobic threats as a way of policing other boys' and men's behavior. The message is clear: if you act in a way that is considered inappropriately masculine (in this case, talking about your prostate), you will be punished by being accused of being gay or feminine.

As I watched all of this unfold, I was stunned. The part of me that is concerned about men's well-being wanted to take Sal's situation seriously and ask him how he was doing. Did he have the results, what did he know about prostate biopsies, and so on. But the part of me that is a man, and knows firsthand what public silencing can feel like, was ultimately stronger. The truth is that I was afraid that if I spoke up, the shame and humiliation would be turned my way. So I did what many boys and men do when they see other men going through this kind of thing. I stared at the ground, shuffled my feet, and tried not to laugh, even though I ultimately did when it became apparent that I was not joining in. Such is the power of public silencing in men's lives.

When we finally hit all of our shots and left the tee, I walked up to Sal and asked him how it was going after having had the biopsy. He brushed me off by saying that it was no big deal, but I persisted and asked if he had gotten the results. Our conversation went like this:

ME: Do you have the results yet?

SAL: No, I am not sure that I want to know.

ME: Man, that's a tough one. I'd have had a hard time focusing on my golf game, at least more than usual!

SAL: Yeah, it stinks all right. But what are you going to do? Hope for the best, try not to complain.

Again, "can't complain." Still, I had tried, however ineffectively, to give him a chance to express his vulnerability.

Imagine what it felt like to be Sal, out for a round of golf with his friends. After the incident on the tee he now had three problems. First, he had just had a prostate biopsy for which he did not have the results and about which he was understandably worried. Second, Sal had been humiliated and shamed by his friends for revealing his concerns. And finally, he now had to finish six more holes of golf (about two hours) with this same group of men while simultaneously

- coping with his own worry about his situation;
- coping with his own feelings of humiliation and shame following Fred's comments;
- laughing it off and being an "easygoing guy"; and
- trying to play decent golf to avoid additional shame and criticism.

### Shame

I mentioned shame several times in relating Sal's story because shame is one of the major consequences of excessive public silencing. Shame is different from guilt. Guilt occurs when people disapprove of their own actions. Shame occurs when people experience a very deep and profound feeling of self-dislike, along with the impulse to run away or hide from others. When people feel ashamed they experience themselves as outcast, unworthy, and somehow having broken the norms of groups or individuals that are important to them. As we will see in chapter 4, many men experienced intense feelings of shame as children when they let their vulnerability be seen by others. The result is that perceived weaknesses, desires for help, or otherwise painful feelings tend to be kept private. This privacy only makes the feelings of shame about one's own vulnerability more intense, which, in turn, feeds the tendency toward personal and private silence.

Boys and men do not necessarily need to be publicly silenced directly by peers in order for shame to keep them from expressing their vulnerability. There is a tremendous amount of learning that goes on in a man's lifetime simply by watching what happens to others and trying to avoid a similar fate. Movies, television, and video games play a particularly powerful role in this regard. In their book *Packaging Boyhood*, the researchers Lyn Mikel Brown, Sharon Lamb, and Mark Tappan review decades of studies focusing on the impact of media representations of masculinity on boys' and young men's development.[12] They conclude that the range of acceptable behavior in images of jocks, superheroes, nerds, and other iconic figures is very narrow. Particularly in teen movies (e.g., *The Breakfast Club, Stand by Me, American Pie*), boys who make the mistake of showing their real vulnerability are subject to, at best, mocking and, at worst, profound humiliation. Therefore, many young boys live with the chronic fear of being publicly silenced should they reveal their true fears, worries, desires for intimacy, or other vulnerable feelings.

## PUTTING IT ALL TOGETHER: THE CYCLE OF SILENCE

The invisibility of men's pain is continuously reinforced by a cycle of personal, private, and public silence. (See the accompanying figure.)

## THE CYCLE OF SILENCE

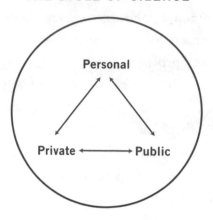

The cycle can start anywhere, but once it gets going it is hard to break. For example, when men keep their pain and vulnerability private, it is hard for others to know what is really going on. Others are then more likely to create the experience of public silence for men because they do not ask about men's lives (a sort of pervasive "don't ask, don't tell" policy with regard to men's vulnerability). When men experience public silence they are more likely to keep things private because it is safer that way. If they keep their emotional lives private for long enough, they may end up being personally silent, simply because they rarely if ever have the opportunity to identify and communicate what they are truly feeling.

When this cycle goes on long enough, it can begin to feel like an inescapable trap. In some cases, the end result is truly a crisis situation. One of my former students shared with me a graphic story that I will never forget, about a man she knew—we'll call him Eric.

### Eric's Story

Eric was working in a high-pressure financial environment; the type with all the cubicles, phones constantly ringing, and employees running their fingers through their hair. Over time the pressure mounted for Eric until he felt like he was going to break. This sort of intense pressure in the work environment is very common, particularly in the current economic circumstances. (Just like in the 1930s, the newspapers are increasingly filled with stories of men committing suicide due to what seem like insurmountable economic problems.)

Eric did not take his own life. Nor did he take the afternoon off, share his situation with friends or coworkers, or visit his primary care physician or a counselor. He kept the problems to himself. When Eric finally reached the point where he felt like he was going to explode, he got up from his desk, walked toward the front of the office, and hurled himself through a heavy plate-glass door. Needless to say, he suffered countless serious cuts and bruises and was taken to the emergency room.

As I listened to this story, I was shocked and horrified that someone could endure so much private pain that it would lead them to see no other option but to jump through a plate-glass door. I also could not help but notice that his actions were extremely public and seemed to cry out, "Look at me! I am in pain here and I need help!" But what really blew me away was what happened next. Eric returned to work after a few days, and *no one said a word to him about what happened.* No one asked how he was doing, no one expressed concern, and no one offered to talk if he needed to. It was as if the whole thing never took place. The message Eric received was ultraclear: what you did was so unacceptable, so *shameful,* and so weak that we will not talk about it. Now this man had two sets of problems: the ones that initially led him to cry out for help, and the fallout from breaking the silence, for he bore the scarlet letter of someone who couldn't handle the pressure and "broke."

## JUST TALK ABOUT FOOTBALL

The effects of the cycle of silence are not always so dramatic. But they can still have powerful effects on a man's life at crucial times. And this is true not just for men who tend to have trouble with emotions. You would think that as a psychology professor— particularly one who studies men's lives—I would have this all figured out. Well, think again. I want to share the following story with you to show just how pervasive these processes are and how they can come into play at important times in a man's life.

My daughter was born September 28, 2001, just two weeks after 9/11. Needless to say, the weeks leading up to her birth were filled with uncertainty. In addition to the normal anxiety all parents go through during pregnancy and birth, my wife and I were experiencing the fear and uncertainty that affected all Americans following the tragic events of 9/11. Like many parents-to-be, we attended a series of birthing classes, and they continued until the day before our daughter was born. The classes occurred in groups of anywhere from four to eight couples who had no relationship with each other except for the fact that they were all expecting a child. The majority of the time was spent on the nuts and bolts of the birthing process. The instructor focused primarily on women's bodies and exactly how a baby makes it from the womb to the world.

Periodically, I would glance at the men in the room and try to gauge their emotional state. None of them looked comfortable.

Most were sitting up in their chairs and staring straight ahead. And I was certainly not comfortable myself. The images of a child being born were terrifying; I simply couldn't imagine my wife's body doing that. And if it did, I wasn't sure I could handle watching it. When you combined this with the general fears about fathering that most men experience around the birth of their first child, it all added up to a pretty healthy dose of anxiety.

But we weren't talking about any of that. When we talked about the men in the room, it was about how they could be of help to their partners during the birthing process. In other words, we were reestablishing the "provider-supporter" role for the men, and in the process we all complicitly agreed that talking about what the men were experiencing was off limits. Don't get me wrong. The process of giving birth to a child is extremely stressful for women. It is impossible to compare it directly to what it is like for a man to participate in the process. I'm certainly not suggesting that men's fears are equal to women's. But I am quite certain that many, if not all, men feel very helpless and concerned during the process of labor, and they are given virtually no tools to deal with it. Encouraging their partners to "breathe, breathe, breathe . . ." only helps men by giving them something to do, and often it is of little or no help to their partners.

Toward the end of the last birthing class, the instructor divided the women from the men. The other men and I went into a separate room, where we sat in a circle and waited awkwardly for the instructor to arrive. We had never been encouraged to talk to each other for even a few minutes, despite the fact that we were all going through a similar set of extremely powerful experiences—most of us for the first time. So here we were, eyes shifting from one to another, not sure what was expected of us. In time, the instructor arrived. She asked us to spend about fifteen minutes discussing our fears and concerns about the process of having a child and to make a list to share with the women. Then, as she left the room, she put her head back through the door and joked, "Really, you can discuss football for most of the time and then jot a few things down at the last minute." We all chuckled nervously, looked quickly at each other, and proceeded to discuss how the New England Patriots were doing that season. What else could we do at that point? Then, with a couple of minutes left, one guy reminded us that we would look pretty dumb if we did not have a list when we rejoined the women. Unfortunately, we never got to it. But if we had, our list might have looked something like this:

- What if I can't handle watching the delivery of the baby and have to leave the room? Will my partner think less of me?
- What if the sight of my wife's body giving birth is physically disgusting to me and it affects how desirable I find her in the future?
- What if she is in so much pain that there's nothing I can do? What if I fail to help her?
- What if I do not feel love for the baby right away? What would that mean about me?
- What if my wife and baby die during the process?

These are the real fears, the silent fears. No one talked about them.

## THE BOTTOM LINE: FLEXIBILITY IS KEY

Clearly it is not healthy to keep all of your problems to yourself, all of the time. And it is not helpful to "dump" every little problem you experience onto other people. On the other hand, flexibility and balance are probably the most adaptive strategies. There are times when sharing with others is a critical part of coping with life's ups and downs, and there are times when "sucking it up" and moving on is the right way to go.

People run into trouble when they are so committed to a single approach that they cannot adapt to the demands of the situation. One of the participants in our research, Ryan, stated emphatically that he saw no advantage whatsoever in "burdening" other people with his problems. From a very young age, Ryan had been taught by both of his parents that "people are responsible for handling their own problems. No one wants to hear you whine about yours." When I asked Ryan about the pros and cons of keeping things to himself all the time, he recalled several instances in childhood when he had discussed his personal life with others, only to later have his confidence betrayed. He clearly saw no upside to making his inner life more visible to others. Given that I had not known this man for very long, I was in no position to challenge him on the issue. I could tell that trying to convince him it was a good idea to open up more was not going to get us anywhere. As I thought about it, I realized that I was experiencing part of what it was like to be in a relationship with Ryan; the more I pressed him, the more he dug his heels in.

All of our research participants complete a survey about the frequency with which they seek help from various people in their lives. The measure is very specific and asks how often, and for how long, you have sought help from different potential sources of support over the last month. When Ryan completed the survey something very interesting happened. Ryan asked me where he stood in relation to other men in our research. He wanted to know how common was his approach of keeping everything to himself. "Do you have a guess?" I asked. "Well," Ryan said, "I've often wondered if maybe I am a little, or a lot, more private than most people." When we looked at Ryan's answers it became apparent that he was in fact at the lower end of the distribution in his tendency to turn to others when he faced problems in his life. "What do you make of that?" I asked Ryan. "Surprised, but maybe not so surprised," he said. "I guess I am kind of rigid about that." "How is the rigidness working for you?" I asked. Ryan's response to my question revealed much about the importance of flexibility in people's lives.

> It keeps me from being disappointed, that's for sure. I mean, nobody gets the chance to let me down. Nobody gets the chance to tell me what to do about my problems, and overall it feels kind of familiar to handle stuff this way. On the other hand, I have to admit that I do get kind of tired of living in this bubble where nobody knows what is going on. Even my wife is clueless most of the time. I realize that I am probably the poster child for the silent type, and that's not really the way I want to be remembered.

Ryan is a good example of someone who learned a particular way of coping with problems early in life. That approach became so ingrained that he applied it to every situation in his adult life, regardless of the consequences. We all do this to some degree. But when we become so inflexible that we cannot adapt to the demands of different situations, we can run into problems. In Ryan's case, these problems included loneliness, estrangement from his wife, and the fear of dying almost literally "in silence." In talking to him further, I could see that Ryan's rigid pattern of keeping problems to himself was creating more problems than the ones he was initially facing.

**HOW TO USE THIS BOOK**

This book is about what you can do as an individual to change things for the better. My goal is to help you understand how men's silence and invisibility work, where they come from, and the problems they can produce. Once you understand these issues you will be in a position to make changes in the way you approach your own emotional life or the lives of the men you love.

Both men and women stand to benefit from reading this book. Women will learn how to better recognize when the men they love are struggling and what they can do to help. Exercises scattered through the book will help women understand their own attitudes toward men's inner lives, assess how silence and invisibility might be affecting their relationships with men, and develop more effective ways of communicating with men about difficult topics involving vulnerable emotions such as sadness, fear, anxiety, grief, and depression.

Women may also find that some, or many, of the descriptions of silence and invisibility in men's lives apply to them as well. This shouldn't be surprising. Both women and men are, first and foremost, human beings; they have much in common. Plus, as women continue to experience increased power and visibility in society, they naturally take on some of the roles, activities, and ways of thinking that have traditionally been considered masculine.

Men can learn a lot about themselves by reading this book. It does not provide an X-ray of individual men's minds, and I do not pretend to know the causes of individual men's behavior. However, I do have a few general road maps, and I've spent a long time surveying the terrain. I suspect that most men will see a part of themselves in the book and may find the road maps helpful for making sense out of some potentially complex territory. For example, men will learn why they are so prone to keep quiet when things get difficult, and how they can talk to others about what is going on in their lives without losing face, so to speak. The exercises for men will not only help them understand their own attitudes toward sharing their lives with others, but also provide opportunities to explore their beliefs about what it means to be a man, and how these beliefs might be helping and harming them in different areas of life. I also discuss methods for developing more effective ways of communicating what is actually going on emotionally during difficult or stressful times.

Finally, couples may wish to read this book together, and to share their thoughts about the exercises with each other. I never fail to be amazed at how common it is for partners in a relationship to *think* that they understand everything about each other's attitudes and perceptions regarding the major issues in the relationship. Of course, men's silence and invisibility are common issues in relationships, and I have seen countless instances of misunderstandings about men's intentions when they keep quiet, their partner's feelings about it, and so on. Working through this book together will help partners in a relationship to see when their take on things is similar, and when they are reading things quite differently. Some of the exercises are designed to help couples communicate more effectively about men's inner lives.

## A PREVIEW OF THINGS TO COME

In the remainder of this book I will help you to understand how silence and invisibility operate in men's lives. I will also show you where the problem comes from and what you can do about it. In part 2 I describe the impact of men's silence and invisibility on well-being in the domains of physical health, emotional health, relationships, and friendship. In part 3 I move back to the bigger picture and consider how men can continue to be seen and heard when they face setbacks in life. The final chapter of part 3 focuses on larger societal changes that must occur if we are going to continue to open our eyes and ears to the realities of men's inner lives.

# 2

# The Causes of Silence and Invisibility

## AN ALL-TOO-COMMON STORY

I recently heard a story that is all too common in the lives of men. While having some work done on my house I met Jim, a forty-four-year-old carpenter who came highly recommended by good friends. I hired him, and over several weeks Jim and I began to chat about things the way men often do (sports, music, carpentry, and so on). Eventually we got to talking more in depth about our jobs, and I mentioned that I was writing a book about the silence that often surrounds the pain in men's lives. Jim laughed and said, "Pain and silence? Have I got a story for you!" He proceeded to tell me about an injury that he suffered as a child and the events that followed.

When I was about five years old, I remember crashing my Big Wheel and busting open my chin. Every kid does it at some point, I'm sure. But it wasn't the injury that hurt the most. It was what happened after. My dad took me to the hospital, and the doctor had to sew it up. I remember that he (the doctor) put some sort of cloth over my face so I couldn't see what was happening. It covered my whole face, including my eyes. My dad was sitting right next to me as the doctor was working, and I remember at one point I could feel something sharp hitting something very hard in the middle of my chin. The pain was like nothing I'd ever felt before. Every time the doctor did that I felt these electrical pulses running from my face down through my whole body. I had tears streaming down my face under that cloth, but I kept quiet and did not say anything. When the doctor pulled the cloth off my face and saw me crying he said, "Why didn't you say something?! I must have been hitting the bone."

When I asked Jim why he *did not* say anything, he said:

"I don't know [laughing]. I guess it just didn't seem like I was allowed to. First, it was my fault that I busted my chin open, so why should I be allowed to cry about it? Plus, my dad was sitting right there, and the last thing I wanted was for him to see me bawling. I guess I've always been like that."

Jim's story is striking for a number of reasons. First, it is all too common. The majority of the men I have spoken with in our research studies relay similar stories when the topic of keeping emotions under control comes up. Second, the cloth over Jim's face is a perfect metaphor for the hidden pain that so many men experience. And Jim's powerlessness to speak during the procedure is analogous to many men's inability to *recognize* that they have silent and invisible suffering, much less communicate about it. Finally, when Jim told me the story, there did not seem to be a trace of emotional or physical pain in his recollection of the events; in fact, he laughed about them. Like many adult men, Jim now saw his own traumatic conditioning during childhood as normal, even humorous.

You might be thinking, well, of course these sorts of things happen in childhood. Children, and especially boys, need to learn to keep their emotions in check and to not start bawling every time they are in pain. Of course that's true on some level. It can be very adaptive to keep one's emotions under control, and to inhibit tears under the right circumstances. But it can also place people under tremendous amounts of unnecessary stress when the fear of being shamed, criticized, or rejected keeps a person from sharing what is really going on.

At the risk of stating the obvious, men are not born this way. They do not come into the world hiding their feelings from others. In fact, research on very young infants indicates quite the opposite; on average, boys are more emotionally expressive than girls.[1-4] Slowly, over time, many of these emotionally expressive, sensitive young boys become brittle, silent, and invisible men whose inner vulnerabilities remain hidden.

## THE SCIENCE OF MEN'S SILENCE
## AND INVISIBILITY

Where is all this silence and invisibility coming from? This is a critical question if we truly want to address the problem. It also turns out to be an enormously complex question to try to get a handle on scientifically. Genetics, economics, gender studies, social psychology, and many other disciplines all have something to say when questions related to gender arise. I am not going to pretend to provide you with a definitive account of why men keep their problems to themselves. Rather, I'll present a broad overview of different theories and bodies of evidence. But before doing so, I want to say a few words about the particular point of view that informs the way I interpret existing theories and research.

First, I am a clinical scientist. This means that I take seriously the role of scientific evidence in decision making. At the same time, I am convinced that when it comes to the social sciences there are few if any facts that exist free from the way we interpret them. Put another way, our own preexisting beliefs, values, assumptions, and biases shape what we consider to be good evidence in favor of one theory or another. For this reason, I also place a lot of weight on how *useful* different theories and research findings are; the farther they can go toward solving important human problems, the more attention I am willing to give them. Finally, my approach to psychology is grounded in principles of human learning. In the broadest sense, the psychology of learning is about how experience changes our behavior. My interest in learning flows directly from my interest in change; we can't change those things that are innate to human beings. However, we can make significant changes in what we teach children about appropriate and inappropriate ways to behave, and we can alter the experiences that people have as adults with the goal of creating more adaptive ways of acting in the world.

From a scientific perspective, there are two major approaches to understanding why men's lives are often silent and invisible. Not surprisingly, they divide largely on where they stand on the perennial question of nature versus nurture that has bedeviled psychology since the field's inception. Evolutionary psychology and contemporary neuroscience see the origins of men's behavior as occurring largely in the genetic inheritances our species has developed over centuries of evolution, and also in the resulting specific brain structures and processes that supposedly differentiate men from women.[5-6] In contrast, psychologists who take a social learning perspective begin with the assumption that men's silence and invisibility are largely learned in an individual's lifetime as a result of societal pressures and practices that reward some activities and punish others.[7-8]

In the following sections, I consider each of these theories in some detail. Because I want this book to help readers work more effectively with men's lives, I place a strong emphasis on what each theory can offer in terms of creative and potentially effective ways to solve problems and enhance quality of life in the real world. I also attend to the available scientific evidence to evaluate the degree to which different theories are consistent with the findings from scientific research. As will become clear shortly, there is not nearly enough scientific research available to know definitively which theory has the most support. This is yet another example of the silence and invisibility surrounding men's well-being; remarkably, relatively few professional researchers have considered it a worthwhile field of study.

## THE ANCESTRY OF SILENCE AND INVISIBILITY

Evolutionary psychologists attempt to understand human behavior by examining how certain tendencies that humans have today may have been adaptive in our evolutionary history. A key assumption evolutionary psychologists make is that our brains actually have not changed much compared to those of our hunter-gatherer ancestors. In his book *The Mating Mind*, Geoffrey Miller reviews archaeological evidence showing that the period from roughly 1.6 million to ten thousand years ago was the critical period during which human brains took on their unique characteristics.[9] The best available evidence seems to indicate that not much has changed in terms of brain structure since that time. This suggests that, at the biological level, our basic decision making tendencies vis-à-vis certain critical activities, such as mating, eating, and working together in groups to obtain resources, also have not changed much since that time. However, the nature of our social world (i.e., culture) has changed dramatically. Thus, for an evolutionary psychologist to explain a certain human behavioral tendency, he or she would look to how that tendency was associated with a greater likelihood of survival and reproduction in our human ancestors. If the tendency allowed an individual to survive and reproduce, it would then be more likely to be passed down in our genetic heritage within the human species. This would be true even if that same tendency was not particularly adaptive in modern times.

This perspective has a lot to offer when it comes to understanding men's vulnerability. First and foremost, it suggests that men's tendencies to remain silent and invisible may have offered evolutionary advantages in the past, even though they may be disadvantageous currently, depending on the situation. To get an idea of how this reasoning works, consider the example of sugar and carbohydrates. Many people think that we are facing an epidemic of obesity in modern Western culture. A major part of the problem is our tendency as individuals to consume larger amounts of simple and complex sugars than we really need from a nutritional perspective. Put simply, we seem to crave sweets and carbohydrates. Manufacturers of these foods are well aware of our cravings, so there is much money to be made by supersizing French fries, big-gulping soft drinks, and so on.

But why do we crave these sorts of substances if they are ultimately unhealthy? To say that humans just naturally like sweets does not answer the question. *Why* do we like them so much? An evolutionary psychologist would point out that in the environment in which our modern brains evolved, such foods provided good sources of energy during or between episodes of hunting for more protein-rich foods. Thus individuals who found sugar and carbohydrates appealing were more likely to eat these foods, more likely to survive, and more likely to reproduce, thus passing on that preference to subsequent generations. Those individuals who did not take advantage of sugars and carbohydrates were presumably less likely to survive, and for that reason most of us in the modern world find these foods appealing. In short, our brains have been "wired" through a process of natural selection.

It may seem like a huge stretch to apply the same logic to men's tendency to keep problems to themselves. But this is exactly what evolutionary psychologists are likely to do. How, they ask, did it benefit men in their evolutionary environment of adaptation to keep their vulnerable inner lives hidden from view? Evolutionary psychologists point out that during that time men were in competition for resources that included not only food but also potential reproductive mates. Archaeological evidence suggests that humans cooperated in groups, but at the same time individuals were predisposed to act in ways that maximized their self-interest. The question, then, is whether it was in men's self-interest to keep their vulnerability silent and invisible to the degree that they could.

One possibility is that keeping apparent weaknesses hidden helped individual men to appear fitter for hunting and other cooperative efforts to gain resources. Those men who could appear fit for battle, so to speak, may have been more likely to share in the collective spoils that were generated from hunting, fighting with other groups, and so on. Another possibility is that those men who stayed quiet about their problems appeared more desirable to potential female mates. As a result, they would have been more likely to reproduce and pass on whatever genetic code made individual men more likely to hide their distress.

On the other hand, it is not hard to imagine circumstances under which disclosing that you were unhappy or needed help could be to an individual's advantage in terms of survival and reproduction. If other individuals in your social network responded with tangible support (shelter, resources, etc.), disclosing vulnerability might be associated with greater chances of surviving and reproducing.

This illustrates one of the major obstacles to finding any conclusive scientific evidence in support of an evolutionary perspective: evolutionary psychologists must always interpret and infer what *may have been the case* in the past, and use that to make sense out of what they see in current human behavior. Perhaps more important, other than our most basic survival and reproductive functions, evolution hasn't "hardwired" humans to do anything other than respond flexibly and adaptively to our environments, if at all possible. In other words, there is no keep-men's-inner-lives-quiet gene that we know of. The conditions under which it would be helpful or harmful to keep silent and invisible are so complex that any hardwiring would have to allow for a great deal of flexibility in how it operated.

So if there is no evidence that evolution, genes, DNA, and men's brains are the singular cause of men's tendency to keep their vulnerability to themselves, we have to consider numerous other social, historical, cultural, and psychological factors. At the same time, it seems reasonable to assume that the effects of these more social processes depend, in part, on how they are responded to by individual men. And how men respond depends, at least in part, on how their brains have evolved. The bottom line is that it is very difficult to separate the combined effects of nature and nurture when it comes to complex human social behavior.

## LEARNING THE DOS AND DON'TS
## OF MANHOOD

As I mentioned previously, my particular bias is to focus more on what men learn during their lifetimes about their own vulnerability, and how this affects their behavior in many areas of life. This bias stems in part from my background in psychology, specifically in the intersection between clinical psychology and the basic science of human learning. Social scientists have made tremendous progress in understanding how our thoughts and behaviors are often learned from our environments. These same thoughts and behaviors have a powerful effect on how we cope with problems in life, how we feel on a daily basis, our risk for developing psychiatric disorders, and so on. Thus, focusing on human learning as a way of understanding men's silence and invisibility is a general approach supported by a great deal of scientific evidence. But above and beyond that, there are practical reasons to focus on what boys and men learn about vulnerability. If we understand when, where, and how such learning takes place, we can change how we go about raising boys, and how we treat adult men when it comes to problems in their lives.

Human beings are remarkably flexible. From a very early age we learn to craft our activities so that our needs get met. In order to do this, we need to be exquisitely sensitive to feedback from our environment. We learn to do things that produce positive consequences in the environment (called reinforcers), and we learn not to do things that produce negative consequences (called punishers). For example, young children learn very quickly that certain behaviors such as crying and fussing tend to be followed by comfort, feeding, a clean diaper, or other positive consequences. On the other hand, criticism and anger are examples of punishers. As children grow they learn not to do certain things that tend to produce anger and criticism from others (e.g., creating a finger-painting masterpiece on the bathroom wallpaper).

This process continues throughout life as we adapt our behavior based on continuous feedback from our environment. At the same time, some of the lessons we learned early in life tend to stick with us, either because the feedback was so intense at the time, or because it was repeated over and over and over again. A good friend of mine, for example, is a very positive person, so much so that she has a hard time allowing herself to feel even slightly down. When she feels natural human emotions, such as sadness, she becomes worried that she won't be able to escape from these feelings, or that she is doing something wrong by not being more positive. One time I asked her if she ever thought about where this insistence on being positive all the time came from. She thought about it and then said:

> You know, it never occurred to me before, but I remember these signs around the house when I was growing up. They were all embroidered, or needlepointed, or something like that. They said, PRACTICE PLEASANTRY: IT PAYS. My mother and father used to point at those signs whenever one of us got cranky, or whenever there was some sort of argument in the house. And then all the conflict would come to a grinding halt because we knew that if we did not follow the rule things were going to get even worse than they were.

What my friend described is a very clear example of what psychologists call *social learning*; she learned from her social environment (in this case, her parents) a powerful rule about what to do with negative feelings. The rule was not to express the negative feelings, and to express positive ones because the environment will reward you if you do ("it pays"). The point of this example is not that the rule is inherently good or bad. Sometimes it does pay to practice pleasantry, and other times it does not. It all depends on what you are trying to achieve in a particular situation and what the risks and potential benefits are. My point is more basic and far-reaching. Much of what governs our current behavior are past experiences where certain actions were followed by positive consequences and others were followed by negative consequences. This process mostly occurs outside of our awareness. I am not talking about a deep dark unconscious mind that controls us, but rather suggesting that the majority of what we do we do because over time we've been taught to do it by those around us.

A human being's status as either male or female has a powerful and long-lasting effect on what he or she learns about appropriate and inappropriate behavior. Gender norms are the dos and don'ts that boys and girls, and men and women, learn about what society considers appropriate and inappropriate for their gender.[10-11] These norms are transmitted to us from our social environment, and the process begins at an extremely early age. The stereotype of automatically selecting blue clothes and decorations for boys and pink for girls is one good example. But these norms extend far beyond how boys and girls should dress or decorate their rooms. In most Western societies men are expected to:

Keep their emotions under control

Handle problems on their own

Avoid anything considered too feminine or "gay"

Be physically strong

Take control of situations

Be a risk taker

Be financially successful

It is easy to see how these norms can influence all aspects of boys' and men's lives. Research has shown that both parents and peers teach children about gender norms. The effects begin very early in a child's life. In one classic study, adults were presented with an infant they had never met. In half the cases they were told that it was a boy, and in the other half they were told it was a girl. In all cases the sex of the baby was the same. The adults were then asked to describe the infant's personality. When they were told that it was a boy, they described the infant as energetic, funny, confident, and so on. When they were told it was a girl, they described it as sweet, loving, et cetera. These findings demonstrate that adults are likely to project their own expectations for appropriate gendered behavior onto young children, and to do so in ways that are consistent with their stereotyped expectations.

There is also evidence that gender socialization plays a role in how boys and men learn to experience, express, and respond to a wide range of emotions. The effects of such socialization are likely to continue through adolescence into adulthood. For example, findings from studies of child and adolescent coping strategies indicate that boys are more likely than girls to use strategies that involve avoidance of negative feelings.[12–16] The ways in which boys and men respond to negative feelings are influenced by culturally prescribed gender norms that discourage expression of "soft" emotions such as sadness and fear and encourage expression of "hard" emotions such as anger. For example, a recent study demonstrated a 50 percent decrease in boys' expressions of sadness and anxiety from preschool to early school age. Parental responses to emotion, particularly those of fathers, were associated with this decrease over time.[17] This emotion socialization has been linked to the development of externalizing problems such as substance abuse and aggression.[18–19]

Both boys and girls tend to be punished for violating gender norms, although the evidence suggests that boys who do so are evaluated much more negatively. This is not surprising since the popular terms for girls who violate feminine norms (e.g., *tomboy*) are less derogatory than those for boys who violate masculine norms (e.g., *wimp, fag*). By adolescence, young boys are extremely attuned to masculine norms and are typically heavily invested in keeping themselves and others in line with them. I often use the term *policing masculinity* to describe the tendency most boys have to punish other boys who step out of line by violating masculine gender norms. This punishment often takes the form of ridicule or shaming, as when young boys who shed tears on the playground are called *sissies, wimps, pussies,* and so on. In its more extreme form this policing can also result in violence, as when gay men are physically attacked simply because, by virtue of identifying as homosexual, they are violating a powerful masculine norm.

The policing of masculinity is not limited to the playground, and adult men need not identify as homosexual to experience its effects. One recent event from my own life illustrates well just how pervasive this process is. A few years ago I was asked by National Geographic to provide commentary for a TV documentary the network was creating on a group called the Dog Brothers. This group engages in a form of martial arts that is quite violent and includes fighting with wooden knives and sticks. When these men meet to fight they report feeling very close to each other, and very alive; at the same time, it is not uncommon for the battles to end in injury and bloodshed. Watching film footage of their events reminded me of a real-world example of the popular film *Fight Club*. As noted earlier in this book, the first rule of fight club is "don't talk about fight club." I was soon to be reminded that the rules of masculinity are quite similar.

As a social scientist who studies men, I was certainly familiar with the notion that competition and physical confrontation can make men feel good about themselves. However, as someone interested in the way masculine norms affect men's well-being, I took a critical stance toward the group's practices and commented in the documentary that it was unfortunate that there are not more adaptive ways for men to develop close relationships with each other that do not involve these sorts of traditionally masculine battles. The day after the film first aired nationally I received the following unsigned e-mail message.

Dear Sir:

I could not believe how much of a pumpkin boy you allowed yourself to be portrayed as on the Nat Geo special last night. Have you not even an ounce of testosterone in you? Do you give little boys dolls and nurse outfits to play in?

From now on when anybody asks me what is wrong with this country, I have only two words to say: Michael Addis.

The first thing I want to point out about this e-mail is that I have no idea what a "pumpkin boy" is, although I am sure it's not good. I also noticed the tremendous amount of anger that comes across; it clearly disturbed this person that I would question how helpful it is for men to engage in violent combat as a way of feeling connected to each other. The anger is clearly directed toward me and is intended to punish and shame me for violating masculine norms. And in fact I did feel ashamed upon first reading the message. The feeling was very distinct and similar to that sense of humiliation and rejection that young boys experience when they shed tears on the playground. This is a good example of policing masculinity, and it points out that you do not have to get too far out of line before somebody, somewhere, will remind you what the rules of manhood are and pull or push you back into line.

## WHAT IS MASCULINITY?

Talking about policing masculinity begs the question, what exactly is *masculinity*? It is an extremely important question because this is a concept that is widely used by both professionals and laypeople as an explanation for men's behavior. How often have we heard statements such as "He acts that way because he is so masculine"; "Masculinity makes men keep their feelings to themselves so they'll look tough"; "Masculinity is what makes men men." The list goes on. Perhaps not surprisingly, masculinity is often the first thing people think of when they begin to think about men's psychology.

To get a sense of how powerful the concept of masculinity is, I would like to share with you an exercise that never fails to raise a few eyebrows when I use it in public speaking settings. The goal of this exercise is to get you thinking about how you think about men and masculinity. You may not even know that you *do* think about men and masculinity. But if you have grown up in Western society, or any society for that matter, you have developed a way of thinking about these concepts. It is simply unavoidable.

In order to complete the exercise, all you have to do is read two different statements and then think about the first words that pop into your mind. It is very important that you not look ahead to the second statement until you have completed the first one. Do not think about your responses too much at all. The goal is to get your first impressions because they typically reflect the most automatic or immediate ideas with which you are working.

Begin by taking a moment to clear your mind. Then read the first statement:

Men are: (what comes to mind?)

Now complete the second statement:

Masculinity is: (what comes to mind?)

I have done this exercise with people countless times, and here are some of the most common responses I have heard.

Men are:

strong
stoic
providers
obsessed with sex
independent

Masculinity is:

machismo
being tough
handling problems on your own
being in charge
keeping a stiff upper lip

When we begin to discuss the exercise people often notice how closely the two sets of responses overlap. What this suggests is that most of us understand men and masculinity very similarly, so much so that we have a hard time separating them. Eventually, someone will say something like "Isn't masculinity what makes men men?" or "Isn't masculinity what distinguishes men from women?"

In your own mind you may not have described men and masculinity so similarly. If not, you are one step ahead of the game in working toward decoupling them. In contrast, when most people think about masculinity they imagine some inner essence that makes men manly. Put another way, masculinity is assumed to be those physical, psychological, and social characteristics that make men behave the way men do. But this way of thinking about masculinity is very different from the approach taken by most social scientists. Psychologists, sociologists, and anthropologists do not see masculinity as some sort of deep inner essence of men. Instead, they see it as a set of beliefs and behaviors that men use to demonstrate that they are in line with whatever the dominant gender norms are at the time. This is typically not a conscious process. The process is much more automatic. As a result of the social learning processes described above, men learn to establish masculinity in order to receive social reinforcement, and to avoid punishment. Thus masculinity is not something inside of men that they possess; it is something they do. This is the way I will be using the term *masculinity* for the remainder of the book.

## THE PRESSURES MEN FACE

As I mentioned previously in this chapter, men face tremendous social pressures to *define and defend themselves as appropriately masculine*. These pressures exist week to week, day to day, and at times, moment to moment. For several decades psychologists and sociologists have recognized the power of gender norms in society.

Gender norms are those cultural "shoulds" and "should nots" that define how men and women should think, act, and feel.

It is not hard to see how gender norms dramatically affect the way men experience, express, and respond to problems in their lives. Consider, for example, a man who is suffering from serious depression but does not recognize it as such. Instead, he attributes his low mood, sleep problems, and difficulty concentrating to "stress," and assures himself that when things at work calm down he'll feel better. He chooses not to share his difficulties with friends and coworkers because he doesn't want to appear whiny. My colleagues and I have met countless similar men in our research studies, and I suspect that readers also find this sort of approach to problems familiar in men.

We teach boys, starting from a very young age, that it is inappropriate to talk to others about problems in life. This message continues on into adolescence and adulthood. Adolescent boys and adult men see precious few models of males reaching out to others in times of need or forming meaningful social connections for support through difficult periods. As a result, we are shocked when seemingly normal men act out with rage and violence toward others or take their own lives. We fail to comprehend why returning veterans are unwilling to seek help for post-traumatic stress symptoms, despite being severely depressed and estranged from their loved ones.

## INDIVIDUAL DIFFERENCES

Not all men keep their vulnerability to themselves. Nor do all men have trouble asking for help, and not all men are emotionally stoic. In fact, many men choose *not* to conform to gender norms when they face problems in their lives. Some of these men are famous (e.g., former NFL quarterback and sports commentator Terry Bradshaw, former *60 Minutes* host Mike Wallace). Some have achieved great things in their lives that are consistent with traditional masculine norms, such as fame, financial success, and physical prowess. But when it comes to their emotional well-being, they choose not to stay silent and invisible. Instead they let their vulnerability be seen and heard.

Perhaps these men are somehow fundamentally different. Maybe they are wired differently from men who stay silent and invisible. But I don't think that's really the case. The fact is that many men can cry, ask for help, share their problems with others, and express their emotions, *under the right circumstances*. At the same time, it comes more naturally for some men than for others. This suggests that there are both individual differences and situational influences that affect the way men deal with their own vulnerability. In many ways this is good news because it means that there is a great deal of variability in how men actually behave when it comes to dealing with problems in their lives. We can capitalize on that by identifying the conditions that allow men to actually open up when it would be helpful to do so. In fact, much of the second part of this book is about learning to create exactly those conditions. Being able to see them requires us to think differently about why men do what they do. Rather than seeing men as hopelessly trapped by a bunch of restrictive rules ("tough it out, keep a stiff upper lip," etc.), we need to see men as constantly responding to pressures in their lives in ways that are more or less helpful, depending on the situation. Put another way, we need a different understanding of what gender is, and how it operates, before we can begin to free men from excessive silence and invisibility.

## IT'S IN THE AIR AND EVERYWHERE:
## GENDER AS AN IMPROVISED PLAY

The things that are closest to us, those that surround us day to day, minute to minute, are often the most difficult to see. Gender is exactly like this. My colleague Christopher Kilmartin often says that gender is "in the air." He uses this metaphor to challenge our intuitive assumption that gender is something inside of people, such as a personality characteristic, a set of biological traits, and so on. Instead, his metaphor suggests that gender is a set of social processes that occurs all around us. Much like air, it is something that is simultaneously everywhere and very difficult to see unless you are aware of it.

In addition to seeing gender as in the air, I view the word *gender* as a verb rather than a noun. Gender has more to do with human action unfolding in a social environment than it has to do with personality traits, genetics, or other presumably internal and stable properties of individuals. The metaphor of an improvised play is helpful in getting your head around this view of gender. Masculinity, for example, emerges when individuals or groups begin to engage in plays that are at least partly about what it means, or should mean, to be a man. Each person involved in the interaction is simultaneously writing the play and also serving as an actor with accompanying roles, scripts, and so on. To some degree we are free to make it up as we go along; the meaning of masculinity can change over the course of history, over the course of a conversation, or in a matter of seconds, depending on how each player in the drama approaches his or her role. At the same time, it is very difficult to make up an entirely novel play; we tend to follow each other's leads, and the stories we are able to imagine are heavily influenced by those that have been told previously.

One of my students, Doug, recently described a wonderfully clear example of masculinity viewed from the perspective of a play. Doug worked as an assistant at the art studio at our university. His job was to help other students with their projects by orienting them to the studio, showing them where the supplies were, and so on. One day a young woman walked in and asked for help with her project. Apparently, she began by saying, "I'm hoping you can help me. I'm not very good with power tools." Doug told the rest of the story in his own words.

> It was weird, and very much like a little miniplay we were involved in. As soon as she said she wasn't good with tools, I knew my line was essentially something like "You've come to the right place." I didn't say that exactly, but I knew I *had* to help her, not only because it was my job but because I'm a guy. When a woman says she doesn't know how to use a tool, my role is to know how to use it. So that's what I did. I cut this, glued that, pretended it was all second nature. She smiled, laughed, showed a lot of appreciation. We each knew our roles, and we could pull the whole thing off without thinking about it. Actually, it wasn't until about ten minutes into it that it started to dawn on me, "Is that what Addis means by gender being an improvised play?"

What I am suggesting here is that masculinity is not some biological or psychological property of individual men. Instead, masculinity is something that is acted out in a wide variety of settings with different characters, different plot lines, and different things at stake. Common to all of these improvised plays is a need for individuals or groups to mark men as behaving in ways that are consistent with the way masculinity is understood in a particular cultural context. I am not at all suggesting that the nature of a "play" somehow makes all of this masculine activity inauthentic or insincere. In fact, people are often largely unaware of what they are doing when they engage in a gender play simply because it feels like second nature. Moreover, we all participate in these plays whether we want to or not. Not only are they part of our collective social history, but they also figure in how we learn to behave from family members and peers as we develop.

On the other hand, some people are more prone to engage in such plays than others. To begin with, some are simply more sensitive to potential gender cues in the air. It could be their genetic inheritance, their upbringing, or some combination of the two. Some men, for example, are much quicker to become competitive among a group of men. It is tempting to conclude here that the social learning and evolutionary theorists are right. It must be all in the genes or all about how you were raised. But note that men's behavior, like everyone else's, is extremely sensitive to differences in context. Not all seemingly competitive men will respond competitively in all situations. And even the most self-reliant man will ask for help under the right conditions.

So what makes people engage in gender plays in some situations and not in others? To begin with, some situations are more highly gendered. Remember your first boy-girl dance? Such situations are rich with gender roles, norms, and expectations. In other situations the air is less densely filled with gender. Whether a play will emerge depends on the particular sensitivities individuals bring to the situation and what is "in the air."

## THREE PSYCHOLOGISTS GO SURFING

Whenever I think about this approach to understanding gender, there is one story that quickly comes to mind. It illustrates just how powerful the social environment can be in setting off a gender play, even among individuals who should be the most resistant to the process.

The American Psychological Association (APA) is the largest professional organization of psychologists in the world. Because it is so large, the APA is broken down into more specialized divisions. Division 51 is titled the Society for the Psychological Study of Men and Masculinity and is composed of roughly five hundred members, professionals and students, all of whom are interested in understanding societal and psychological influences on men's well-being. I think it's also fair to say that members of Division 51 are dedicated to transcending traditionally restrictive masculine norms and leading more flexible lives, unconstrained by more machismo-oriented notions of manhood.

Every year the APA holds an annual conference, and several years ago it took place in Oahu, Hawaii. I attended the four-day conference that year and on Saturday afternoon found myself with several free hours in which to explore. I had seen an advertisement the previous day for surfing lessons (all levels welcome!) and was deciding whether to give it a try when I bumped into my colleague Eric and a graduate student with whom he worked named Ray. Both of them seemed intrigued by the idea, so we set off toward the beach. It was a gorgeous sunny day, and I had the sense that we were all looking forward to a new experience and the kind of connection that comes through shared activities and adventures.

Eric was a few years younger than me and seemed to be in good physical shape. Ray was even younger and had worked as a personal trainer before starting graduate school. We each signed a disclosure/consent form indicating that we would not hold the surfing company responsible should something go wrong. There was also a brief survey in which we provided personal information about ourselves. The first question was "What kind of physical shape are you in?" The options were "Poor," "OK," "Good," and "Excellent." Ray was first in line, and I watched him complete the survey while Eric looked over his shoulder. As Eric went to fill his out, I peeked at his response to the first question and noticed that he had circled "Excellent." Without hesitating, I did the same. In actuality, I hadn't been to the gym in close to a year and was not in the least bit prepared for what lay ahead. Nonetheless, I succumbed to the pressure to portray myself as appropriately masculine among my younger colleagues. After all, what could happen?

Our surfing instructor, whom we have since nicknamed Colonel Dude, appeared to be in his midtwenties. His body physique was extremely muscular, and he quickly informed us that he had recently gotten out of the military and had been an avid surfer since he was a child. "I notice you're all in great physical shape here, and that's a good thing," the Colonel said. "We've got a little over a quarter-mile paddle out to the break." I remember thinking that a quarter of a mile didn't seem very far. On the other hand, a nagging sense of uneasiness, which had begun shortly after I effectively lied about my fitness, continued to creep up on me.

After a brief on-shore tutorial we set out for the waves. I had surfed a few times as a teenager and was somewhat familiar with techniques for paddling. The movement takes a great deal of strength and stamina in your arms and shoulders. As you lie on your stomach your upper body bends concavely just above the waist, and your shoulders and neck are elevated above the board. You must maintain this position both to propel yourself forward with your arms and to make sure that you can see what's coming toward you. Neither Eric nor Ray had paddled a surfboard before. As a result, my little bit of experience enabled me to glide faster toward the waves. I was proud of myself as I glanced behind me and smiled at Ray and Eric as if to say, "Could anything be better than this?"

About halfway out to the break my arms and shoulders started to get fatigued. After a few hundred more yards they began to feel like aching strands of spaghetti, and all I could do was lie on my stomach and hope a wave did not break on me. Eventually I got up the energy to turn my head around and see how Eric and Ray were doing. Eric looked about like I felt. Ray, on the other hand, looked as if he had just woken up from a refreshing nap. I closed my eyes and felt the soothing sun and saltwater on my face. *Perhaps it's time for some damage control*, I thought. I knew enough about surfing to know that, feeling as spent as I did at that moment, I wasn't going to be able to do it effectively, much less safely. So I decided to stay on my board for a few more minutes and try to regain some energy.

I had hardly begun to rest when I heard a loud "Look out!" ahead of me and opened my eyes to see Colonel Dude barreling down on me atop his board. He screamed at the three of us as he passed by: "What's matter with you guys?! You're not gonna puss out on me now, are you? Come on, guys, step it up." Ray smiled and paddled past me. I turned to look at Eric, and we both rolled our eyes as if to say, "I wonder if this guy knows that he's talking to a bunch of psychologists interested in men and masculinity?" Still, we paddled forward.

When we finally reached the break, again I was out of steam. Gasping for breath and lying on my board, I stammered to the Colonel, "I'm not sure I can do this." "You're kidding me, right?" he replied. "Come on, be a man about it. I'll give you a push." Again I looked at Eric, and again we rolled our eyes. It was only a short time after I inexplicably managed to get my surfboard turned around that Colonel Dude indeed gave me a push. As I felt the wave gather me up, I could hear the Colonel screaming at the top of his lungs, "Paddle! Paddle your ass off, little man!!" Somehow I managed to get to my feet and stay atop the board just long enough to experience a few seconds of actual surfing and scream "Woohooo!!" hoping Eric and Ray could see and hear me. Then I fell off the board, tumbled around in the whitewash, and eventually came up grinning.

When I managed to get myself back on my board I could see that I was a good one hundred yards closer to shore than the Colonel, and I had also drifted quite a bit down shore away from where the lesson began. The Colonel called out to me, "Nice ride! Let's do it again!" I contemplated paddling back out to the break, but my arms were once again feeling like noodles so I decided to head back to shore. I had barely enough energy to paddle three or four strokes before I had to stop and lay my head down on the board. Unfortunately, because of a strong side current, this also meant that for every few yards I got closer to shore I was also several yards farther down the beach from where we started. After what seemed like half an hour I finally made it to shore, where I rolled off the board and collapsed on my back in the wet sand, trying to catch my breath.

Now I needed to carry my board a good quarter mile down the beach back to the surfing school. Beginning surfers typically start off on longer boards measuring some ten to twelve feet in length, and mine was no exception. I was in no shape to tuck the board under my arm, so I propped it on top of my head and trudged off in the wet sand. To this day I cannot believe that I didn't teeter over and collapse on an unsuspecting sunbather, given how crowded the beach was. When I finally approached the surfing school I heard my name: "Hey, Michael, what's up?"

Turning to my left I saw Eric with a big smile on his face. He was about twenty yards from shore, lying on his board and gliding steadily toward the sand. *How did he manage to get this far and not end up way down shore like I did?* I wondered. That's when I saw Colonel Dude's surfboard right behind Eric's. Eric wasn't even paddling; evidently he had managed to secure a tow-in from the Colonel.

Eric, Ray, and I see each other at least once a year, and we always reminisce about Colonel Dude and our surfing adventure. The story is humorous, to be sure, but there is a serious side to it. I had lied about my physical fitness, and Eric has since told me that he did the same. As a result we paid the price in terms of pure physical exhaustion. But we also put our lives in danger. From the moment we completed the survey, on through to the long paddle, and up to the point of heeding the Colonel's admonition not to "puss out," we responded to gender in the air in ways that threatened our well-being. Remember that all three of us had spent years working on our abilities to resist the pressures of traditional masculinity. Too often such pressures exert their influence long before people are even aware of their presence.

### Josh's Story

Sometimes gender plays can emerge seemingly out of nowhere and directly affect a man's ability to share his inner life with others. Josh was a thirty-two-year-old married man who came to a research study my colleagues and I were conducting after hearing about it on the radio. When I first met him he told me that he was interested in our research because he had experienced some depression in his life and wondered how serious it was. He thought that perhaps we would be able to tell him how bad things actually were for him, and whether it would make sense for him to seek professional help.

Josh was very curious about our research. This is not uncommon because most people recognize that men's vulnerability is a very important topic that is rarely discussed. Josh seemed intrigued by the idea that we wanted to know how he coped with the problems he faced. At the same time, Josh was very cautious and clearly attuned to the fact that he was at a research university talking to a professor of psychology. He referred to me as "Doctor," "Sir," and "Professor" at various points in our first interview, despite the fact that I was dressed in jeans and a casual shirt and introduced myself as Michael. Early in the interview Josh mentioned that he had gone to a community college and taken some psychology classes, but he also said, "I do not know anywhere near as much as you guys. You are the experts, and that's why I am here."

This all seemed very positive on the face of it. Josh was willing to look at problems in his life, he took an interest in our work, and he seemed willing to hear what we had to say. Yet there was something that troubled me about our interaction right from the start. I had the feeling that Josh's tendency to see me and our research team as authorities was getting in the way of talking more openly about his situation. When I asked him about his depression, for example, he said, "I don't know if it is depression. I mean, I don't want to use the word *depression* incorrectly. I am sure you guys know a ton about this, so maybe you can tell me what's going on." Another time he asked me where I received my Ph.D. When I told him that I had gone to the University of Washington, he responded, "I do not think I could have made it into a place like that."

Some sort of perceived status difference between the two of us was getting in Josh's way, preventing him from being vulnerable enough to share what was really going on in his life. In terms of a play, the research setting, including me, the staff, the university, the consent form, and so on, were all part of a scene that made it very difficult for Josh to avoid doing masculinity in my presence. They seemed to activate the norm of keeping problems to yourself when you are around those who rank higher in status, particularly other males.

As it turned out, the play Josh and I were acting out was similar to those he experienced at home. Josh's wife knew about the problems he was having because he talked openly with her, at least most of the time. Other times, particularly when she suggested that he might benefit from talking to a therapist, Josh shut down immediately. When I asked him why, he said:

> I don't know. You'd think I'd be willing to talk to her about it, but there's something in her tone of voice. She denies it. She says I am overly sensitive, but whenever she says she thinks I might need to see a counselor it is like she doesn't believe I can handle my own problems. Plus, it's not really her business, is it? If I've got depression, or if I have a problem or something, that's my decision to make. I do not need her rubbing it in my face.

To Josh's ear, when his wife suggests that he might go to therapy she unwittingly brings masculinity into the room. For a variety of reasons having to do with his personal history, Josh is sensitive to any indication that he might be failing to live up to his notion of what it means to be a man. If he is not in a situation where he perceives himself to be challenged in that way, he is not defensive and is, instead, more open to the possibility of seeking professional help. But as soon as masculinity is in the room he shuts down.

I think the approach of understanding masculinity as something that occurs in the *transaction between a person and his environment* is much more useful than seeing it as a biological trait or a personality characteristic. First, it helps us make sense out of apparently confusing and contradictory behavior. In Josh's case, if we assumed simply that he was a highly masculine, self-reliant man, how could we understand the fact that he came to our study looking for information on his own emotional well-being? Focusing on the way he and his environment interact allows us to see that, in fact, Josh is quite ambivalent about seeking help. Second, we can see that there are things we can do to increase or decrease Josh's openness to reaching out. For example, anything I did that decreased the power differential between us (using my first name, expressing interest in his ideas about his situation, being very transparent about the goals of our research) also increased his willingness to talk about depression.

Finally, focusing on how men interact with their environment offers a much more change-friendly perspective. We can change the way we talk to men, and we can help men to alter the environments they place themselves in. On the other hand, if we think masculinity is a biological trait or a deeply ingrained personality characteristic, how much change is really possible? There is scant evidence that people can really change their basic personality characteristics, no matter how much intensive therapy they've been through. And so far I have yet to see a drug that alters basic biological aspects of gender. More important, if there was one, I suspect that very few men would be interested in taking it.

## MOVING FORWARD

Among the advantages of focusing on human learning as a way of understanding men's silence and invisibility, the most important, to me, is that this perspective is simultaneously compassionate and empowering. It is compassionate because it recognizes that behavior is often a product of past circumstances as well as current situations. Men do not choose to keep their inner lives hidden out of some evil or selfish need to remain private.

But men are also not victims of past circumstances or current situations. A learning perspective does not let them off the hook, but rather empowers them by putting them squarely at the center of responsibility for changing their world. By *responsibility*, I do not mean a moral obligation. I don't think that men should be punished, criticized, shamed, or otherwise viewed negatively for their difficulties identifying and communicating what goes on inside of them. But men are responsible in the sense of being able to respond more adaptively under the right circumstances. The rest of this book is about identifying those circumstances and the variety of more helpful ways that both men and women can respond to the widespread silence and invisibility that surround men's vulnerability.

· 3 ·

# Silence and Invisibility in Your Life

## OBSERVING WHAT YOU DO

Knowledge is power. You can learn a tremendous amount about yourself by paying close attention to the things you do, where you do them, and the consequences they produce. This simple truth is one of the most significant discoveries of psychological science over the past century. It is also the take-home message of this chapter; the more you know about your own reactions to men's silent vulnerability, the more you can do to enhance the quality of your own life and your relationships with men.

Self-assessment is a key part of this process, and the goal of this chapter is to help you take stock of how men's silence and invisibility may be playing important roles in your life. By the end of this chapter you should be able to answer the following questions:

1.  How common is men's hidden vulnerability in your life?
2.  How is men's silence and invisibility affecting your life?
3.  How are you responding to men's silence and invisibility?

4. What are your beliefs about men and masculinity?

5. What are your values?

Before we start addressing these questions directly, I want to make four points about the process of self-assessment. First, self-assessment is a very common process in many approaches to therapy and counseling, and those approaches that regularly use self-assessment tend to have the most scientific support for their effectiveness. Thus there is a considerable amount of evidence indicating that self-assessment is helpful.[1-3]

Second, not all approaches to self-assessment are equally effective. Depending on how you approach the process, you can learn a lot of new and useful information about yourself, or you can learn very little. You need to shoot for what my colleague Paul Rosen calls *sober self-assessment*. I do not mean that you should avoid drinking alcohol when you take stock of your own behavior (although it is probably not a bad idea to be literally sober at the time). What I mean by *sober self-assessment* is taking a close look at yourself in as objective a way as possible. This means seeing yourself in a way that is only minimally clouded by the sorts of personal biases we all carry with us when it comes to questions about our own thoughts, feelings, and behaviors. As it turns out, this is actually much harder to pull off than it sounds; most of us tend to see ourselves how we want to be seen, rather than how we really are. For example, you might like to think that you are the sort of person who is comfortable seeing and hearing men's inner pain, and perhaps you are. Or maybe, like many people, you think this is true when in fact you are uncomfortable. After all, who wants to think they are not comfortable with other people's pain, particularly people they care about?

Third, self-assessment rarely results in a simple yes/no answer to a question. Most important things in life are just not that simple. Instead, a more helpful goal might be to get a sense of the different ways that silence and invisibility may be affecting you (or not). Consider the following example:

One man who participated in our research completed self-assessments related to his values and his style of coping with problems in life. He ranked family as the most important value in his life and also identified the tendency to keep problems to himself as very common. I asked him how the tendency to keep problems private helped his family, and he identified a couple of different ways. At the same time, he began to question whether it was necessary to keep every problem hidden, and whether the messages he was sending his children about reaching out for help were really in line with the value he placed on family. He did not resolve these issues in one hour, but asking the question was a crucial first step.

Fourth, and finally, self-assessment is not about blame. The goal is not to figure out if you or someone else is at fault for a situation or problem in your life. The goal is to learn more about what is actually going on before you jump in and try to solve the problem or change the situation. Too often people get caught up in trying to absolve themselves of blame, put the blame on others, put the blame back on themselves, and so on. And too often these attempts to determine blame actually make it that much *harder to see what is really going on, regardless of whose fault it is.* This chapter will be much more helpful to you if you can put questions of blame aside for a while and focus instead on gaining a deeper and more accurate understanding of how men's silence and invisibility are operating in your life.

Many of the following exercises in self-assessment take the form of thought activities. I will present you with a question, a statement, or something else to respond to, and encourage you to consider your own thoughts, attitudes, and feelings about the issue. Pay attention both to your immediate reactions and to those that come a little more slowly after you've had some time to think. There are no correct answers, and there are no "trick" questions that try to get at anything other than what you see on the face of it. Remember that the purpose of these exercises is to give you some helpful things to think about. Some of the exercises will be more or less relevant, depending on who you are as an individual.

## QUESTION 1: HOW COMMON IS MEN'S HIDDEN VULNERABILITY IN YOUR LIFE?

If you are a man, take a moment and think about the last few times you faced a significant personal problem. By *significant personal problem*, I mean something that caused you a certain level of personal stress, uncertainty, fear, or sadness. Think of something that lasted for more than a few days. If you are a woman, think of the last few times a man you care about faced such a problem. Once you remember a few situations, you can move on to the next step.

If you are a man, think about what you tend to *do* when you face a significant personal problem in your life. If you are a woman, think of a man or boy you are close to and consider what he typically *does* in such situations. After you've given this some thought, you can look at the list that follows for some common examples of what silent and invisible men tend to do when they face problems.

Silent and invisible men often:

- Say things like "Can't complain"
- Say things like "Suck it up, soldier on, etc."
- Say things like "Why think about X?"

- Shrug their shoulders
- Get quiet
- Roll their eyes

You should be able to tell pretty easily if you or a man you care about tends toward the silent and invisible when it comes to problems in life. If one or more of these behaviors occurs often, there is a good chance that silent vulnerability plays some sort of role in your life. The same is true if several of these behaviors occur less frequently but regularly enough to create a pattern.

Other behaviors can indicate whether a person is experiencing hidden emotional pain:

- Being withdrawn or isolated
- Being quiet
- Drinking too much alcohol
- Excessive anger
- High levels of stress
- Taking too many risks
- Having unexplained physical pains
- Overworking
- Being bored all the time

How common are these behaviors in yourself or in a man you care about? As with the previous list, a pattern can emerge when one or two behaviors are happening frequently, or when several of them are occurring regularly albeit less frequently.

In chapter 1, I described the psychologist Ron Levant's research on alexithymia (*a* = without, *lexi* = words, *thymia* = mood/feeling).[4] As you may recall, Levant and his colleagues have suggested that a large number of men have difficulty knowing what they are feeling, labeling it, and communicating it to others. Men who struggle with alexithymia may also be more likely to keep their inner pain silent and invisible. It is therefore important to consider the degree to which difficulty in identifying and communicating feelings is playing a role in your own life or in the lives of men you love.

Levant and his colleagues developed a questionnaire that measures the extent to which different people experience alexithymia. The following three statements, taken from this questionnaire, focus on personal silence. Read each one and consider how much you tend to agree or disagree with it. You can also look at the statements from the perspective of someone else that you know; perhaps a man in your life who you suspect might be experiencing a good deal of personal silence.

- "I do not think I am upset, but then I get a headache, upset stomach, or stiff neck and then realize that I have been upset."
- "I find it very hard to cry."
- "I am often confused about what emotion I am feeling."

## FOR WOMEN

What do you notice about the man you had in mind when you considered these statements? Does he tend to express emotional pain through bodily aches and pains? Does he have difficulty crying? If several of these statements seem very descriptive of the man you are thinking of, he may be someone who has difficulty knowing what he is feeling. This means that when he says, "I do not know what I am feeling inside," he may actually mean it. This is important information for women. It is quite common and understandable for women to feel put off by a man who responds to a compassionate question such as "How are you feeling?" with a curt "I don't know." When men say that they do not know what they feel, they are not necessarily driven by a desire to avoid intimacy. Nor is this a form of mental illness. As we saw in chapter 2, it is something that some men have been taught to do from a young age. But regardless of whether the cause is nature or nurture, the fact is the same: many men experience a great deal of personal silence when it comes to their inner fears, vulnerabilities, and tender emotions.

## FOR MEN

Does anything stand out in your reactions to these statements? Something may or may not. What sorts of examples of your own behavior can you think of that either do or do not fit these statements? If several of these statements seem to describe you, you may be someone who has difficulty knowing exactly what you are feeling at different times. As I mentioned above, this is not unusual among men, and it is certainly not anything to be alarmed about. If you often have trouble knowing what you are feeling, it may simply be that you have not had much experience attending to that part of your life. Doing so can be tremendously helpful in your relationships with others and for your own well-being.

## QUESTION 2: HOW ARE MEN'S SILENCE AND INVISIBILITY AFFECTING YOUR LIFE?

This question can be challenging because it is asking you how the *absence* of something in your life is affecting you. Many people simply do not *see* that they rarely if ever *see* men's inner lives. A good place to start is by rereading the previous statements about hidden pain and difficulty identifying emotions. For those statements that seemed to apply to you, or to a person you care about, you might ask yourself: what effect is this having on me? Some effects may be positive, and some may be negative. A lot depends on the circumstances.

Here are some effects reported by men I have met through our research.

Keeping problems to myself and handling them on my own tends to:

- Keep me from being too dependent on other people
- Make me feel alone at times
- Make me feel like I have too much responsibility
- Make me wish people knew that things are not really going as well as they appear to be for me
- Keep me from being a downer when I am around other people
- Make it hard for other people to know that I might need help or want to talk sometimes

If you are close to a man who has this tendency, how does it affect you? For example, your responses might look something like those that follow.

When (name) keeps problems to himself, I:

- Feel less close to him
- Worry about how he is really doing
- Feel relieved because I know that I do not have to worry about him

- Want to pressure him into opening up more
- Wonder how close to me he really feels

If you have children in your life, you also want to consider how men's silence and invisibility might be affecting them. Children typically learn from their parents how problems in life are to be approached. Men's silence can send a strong message to children that it is not appropriate to talk about your inner fears, anxieties, and other sorts of painful or vulnerable emotions. Remember that children often learn more from what parents do than what they say. A man might say to his children that it is okay to talk about what is going on in your inner life. But if his children see that he rarely does this himself, they may get the idea that what is really expected is silence.

## QUESTION 3: HOW ARE YOU RESPONDING TO MEN'S SILENCE AND INVISIBILITY?

How you respond to men's silence and invisibility is a crucial part of the process. If you are the partner of a man who tends to keep his vulnerability hidden, what do you say in response to his behavior? Do you accept it as normal? Do you get angry at him because he doesn't open up more? Do you avoid him when you know that he is struggling on the inside? Do you let him know that you are there in case he wants to talk, while still respecting his privacy? Do you try to solve the problems for him, even when he doesn't want to talk about them? Do you pressure him to talk more?

If you are a man, how do you respond to your own hidden pain? Do you avoid thinking about it? Do you do things to take your mind off it? If so, how helpful are these responses (e.g., do they actually help to relieve the pain or at least take your mind away from it)? Do you get angry? Do you drink too much alcohol or use drugs that dull the pain but cause other potential problems? Do you try to stay busy? Do you get depressed?

Perhaps you do many of these things, or perhaps you do none of them. What is important is that you develop a clear sense of not only the presence of hidden pain in your life but also how you respond to it. Some ways of responding can make problems worse, and some can make them better. For example, if you are the partner of someone who struggles with hidden pain, and you pressure him to open up more, you may actually be causing him to shut down. If you are a man who responds to hidden pain by becoming angry and drinking alcohol or using drugs, your responses may be making problems worse by threatening your physical and emotional health or the quality of your relationships with family and friends.

## QUESTION 4: WHAT ARE YOUR BELIEFS ABOUT MEN AND MASCULINITY?

Researchers in the psychology of men and masculinity have spent a good deal of time studying differences between people in the beliefs they hold about the nature of men and masculinity.[5–7] Some people, for example, believe that men should be strong and independent, while others believe that men should be emotionally stoic. Still others believe that "real men" should be financially successful. Most people do not hold on to these beliefs or ideologies in a "yes/no" fashion. Instead, they believe in different ideologies to varying degrees. Growing up in my family, for example, people tended to mostly disagree with the belief that men should be emotionally stoic. However, when it came to competitiveness, there was pretty strong agreement that successful men should be competitive. As it turns out, different beliefs and ideologies tend to go along with different approaches to men's inner lives. Thus, assessing your own beliefs about men and masculinity is a critical part of understanding how you tend to react to men's silence and vulnerability.

Assessing your own beliefs about men and masculinity can be a little tricky. The first thing you have to do is ask yourself how honest you are ready to be with yourself. Part of the challenge here is that it has become somewhat politically incorrect for many people to say that they believe men should be physically strong, emotionally stoic, self-reliant, powerful lovers, and so on. This is particularly true for people who take an interest in psychology and gender. It is as if we are *supposed* to have moved past all of that, even though such beliefs are still very common.

Another challenge is that belief systems do not always show up dressed as belief systems, so to speak. In other words, your beliefs about men and masculinity might not be easily accessible in the form of a statement such as "I believe men should be strong." Your beliefs may become clearer when you look at your own behavior. (If you are a man, do you tend to try to appear strong? If you are a woman or the partner of a man, do you tend to be more comfortable around men who have this trait or characteristic?) One way to get started assessing your own beliefs is to complete the following sentence: Men are . . . , and men should be . . . Your response will tell you a lot about your basic assumptions about the nature of men and masculinity.

Psychologists who have attempted to measure different belief systems about men and masculinity typically come up with something similar to the following list, which, not surprisingly, maps pretty well onto the masculine gender norms I discussed in chapters 1 and 2. They include:

- Avoidance of femininity
- Fear and hatred of homosexuals
- Extreme self-reliance
- Aggression
- Dominance
- Nonrelational attitudes toward sexuality
- Restrictive emotionality

As I mentioned earlier, several of these do not paint the most flattering picture of men and masculinity. Nonetheless, most of us continue to be raised in a society that defines much of manhood in this way. The result is that we can't help but buy into these beliefs and ideologies to some degree. This is why I asked you to be honest with yourself, rather than considering what you think you *should* believe.

If you have given yourself the opportunity to explore your own beliefs about manhood in a nonjudgmental way, patterns are likely to emerge. If you tend to think that men should have several of the qualities listed above, perhaps you were raised in a more traditional family. Or maybe you developed these beliefs based on your own experience as a man or your interactions with different men. On the other hand, you may be someone who disagrees with dominant views of men and masculinity, and your views may be less traditional.

Beliefs about men are neither helpful nor unhelpful by themselves; they simply are what they are. They become important when they influence you to behave in some ways more than others, and it is the consequences of such behavior that matter the most. Researchers have found that this is particularly true when it comes to our reactions to men's emotional lives.[8-11] Although there are always exceptions, studies have shown that people who believe that men should be extremely self-reliant and emotionally restrictive are also more likely to display the following characteristics:

Negative attitudes toward seeking help

Higher levels of depression

Greater discomfort with men's displays of vulnerable emotions

Emotional vulnerability is a quality that our society stereotypically associates with femininity. Thus negative attitudes toward femininity, and toward homosexuality, may lead people to be less tolerant of emotional vulnerability in men. I am not suggesting that agreeing with more traditional notions of manhood automatically makes you intolerant and hostile toward men's emotions. What I am saying is that your own beliefs about men and masculinity are an important part of the overall picture. They influence how you feel about yourself, if you are a man, and how you feel toward men when they act in ways that are consistent or inconsistent with your beliefs.

## QUESTION 5: WHAT ARE YOUR VALUES?

Values are the belief systems that are at the core of our beings. Most people are emotionally invested in their values, so much so that they judge their own and others' behavior according to how well it converges with their values. For this reason, values can be extremely motivating; when our behavior is in line with our values we tend to feel better, more energized, and clearer about what we are doing in our lives. On the other hand, when our behavior conflicts with our values we are more likely to feel ambivalent, self-critical, defensive, and so on.

It seems obvious, then, that the best approach is to always

behave in line with our values. If only life were that simple. We are not usually compelled to articulate our values clearly unless they are somehow challenged. In other words, it is possible to go through much of life with far less than a crystal clear sense of the beliefs in which we are most emotionally invested. Take, for example, a couple in which each partner comes from a different religious or cultural background. Each individual in the relationship may not realize the importance of different values until they have a child. It's not that the different values never existed. Rather, they resided comfortably in the background until they were challenged by difficult questions facing the new parents, such as: In what religion will we raise our child? What language or languages will we speak around the house?

Getting clearer on how our values and our behavior do not go together can be a painful and sobering process. That was certainly the case for one of my clients, whom I'll call Dan.

### Dan's Story

Dan was a middle-aged man who placed a very strong emphasis on being there for his family and children. He made sure to involve himself in his children's activities on the weekend, and he worked hard during the week at a job he really did not enjoy because the pay was good and it provided a comfortable lifestyle for his family. When I met Dan he was struggling with a fairly severe and long-standing episode of clinical depression along with regular panic attacks. Because he did not want to worry his wife and children, he had kept the problems to himself for several years. Eventually it got so bad that Dan was afraid he might lose his job if he did not get help, which is why he came to see me.

Very early in our work together we did a formal values assessment. Being a good father and husband came out on top for Dan.

When I asked him how keeping problems to himself helped make him a good father and husband, he responded that it made him appear strong for his family. Dan also felt proud of the fact that he did not burden them with his pain, which, he said, "is clearly my own problem." I agreed that keeping quiet helped him look strong, and also that it made sense not to *burden* his family. In the back of my mind I continued to wonder why sharing problems with close others in his life would necessarily lead those people to feel burdened. Wasn't it possible that they would feel close to him, relieved, that they would want to help? Nonetheless, I continued to listen empathically to Dan and to do my best to understand what life was like for him. I also tried to take into account the importance that he placed on being a self-contained, independent person.

I then decided to ask Dan if there were ways in which keeping everything to himself was working against the value of being a good father and husband. At first, he looked at me like I was nuts, and said, "Are you saying that I would be a better father if my kids knew that I was depressed and having panic attacks?" "I'm not sure," I said. "I am just getting to know you, and I do not have a sense of that one way or the other. But I am curious if you see any ways in which sharing a bit more about your experience with your wife and your children might actually be good for your family as a whole."

Dan took a deep breath and looked up at the ceiling of my office. He reminded me in that moment of a poker player contemplating his next move. Here is where our conversation went next:

ME: You look like maybe you have thought about this before.

DAN: Yeah, it's a tough decision.

ME: What is tough about it?

DAN: Well, sure, part of me would like to talk to my wife about what is going on, but, to be honest, it seems kind of weak. What is *she* going to do about it? She can't solve the problem. And I don't want to look like I am begging for sympathy. She has enough on her plate.

ME: I can understand your concern about burdening her, and you are clearly working very hard to act in ways that are consistent with the value you place on being a good family man. Out of curiosity, what effect do you think it has on her when you keep everything to yourself?

DAN: What do you mean?

ME: Well, what is it like for her? Does she feel closer to you when you keep things quiet? Does she worry less? Is she happier?

DAN [LAUGHING]: Now that's an interesting question.

ME: How so?

DAN: Well, I guess it's something I never thought about. I just assumed that the right thing to do to be a good family man is to handle stuff on my own. Protect the family, you know what I mean? It's how I was raised, so I've never really questioned it.

As we talked about it further, Dan began to wonder how helpful he was really being to his wife by staying hidden. He realized that, in fact, she often asked him how he was doing and had said a few times recently that she was worried about him. I asked Dan if it was possible that his efforts to keep his problems away from his wife were actually making her worry more. He conceded that this was a possibility. Dan also realized that as much as he was physically present with his children on the evenings and weekends, often he wasn't really mentally engaged. His children, and particularly his teenage son, knew something was wrong but had learned over time that "Dad doesn't like talking about stuff." I questioned whether Dan's children might be learning from him not to talk about problems in life. Dan agreed that this might be the case, and he was understandably concerned given the value he placed on being an emotionally engaged father. Without a clear sense of what his own values were, it would have been very difficult for Dan to see that, in some areas of life, his efforts to pass them along to his children may actually have been backfiring.

## EXERCISE: WHAT ARE YOUR VALUES?

You might find it helpful to jot down your values on a piece of paper. Think of those things that are most important to you, and the particular people, experiences, goals, and ideals that motivate you. To get you started, here is a list of a few common values. (Some may be personally relevant for you and others not.)

- self-improvement
- family
- wealth
- love
- children
- self-reliance
- honesty
- kindness
- spirituality
- physical health
- happiness
- intelligence
- humor

What about your own values? Any surprises there? Most people who do this exercise are struck with both the familiarity and novelty of some of their values. Either way, this exercise will help you to consider how consistent your approach to men's silence and invisibility is with your values. For men, you can ask yourself how your approach to your own inner life, or the way you react to other men's inner lives, is helping you to achieve those things you value. If you value self-improvement and independence, for example, and you are someone who prefers to keep things quiet and handle problems on your own, this approach may be in line with the importance you place on independence. On the other hand, keeping quiet may conflict with the value you place on self-improvement. Again, there is no right or wrong here. The important question is how your approach to your own emotional life is helping or hindering you from achieving the things that you value.

If you are the partner of a man, the question becomes: how is your approach to men's inner lives consistent or inconsistent with your own values? For example, does the value you place on family lead you to take a strong interest in breaking the silence and invisibility that affect the man you love? Or does it lead you to subtly encourage him to "be strong" when he faces problems so he can be a good provider?

## PUTTING IT ALL TOGETHER

Now is a good time to take a step back and consider your self-assessment process as a whole. At this point you should have a general sense of how men's silence and invisibility are affecting your life. You should be able to answer such questions as: How am I responding to men's silence and invisibility? What consequences are my responses producing for myself and others in my life? What are my beliefs about men and masculinity, and how are these beliefs influencing the way I react to men's vulnerability? What are my own values, and to what degree am I behaving in ways that are consistent or inconsistent with them?

For many people who undergo this process of self-assessment, certain patterns in their own beliefs and behavior begin to emerge. Whether you fit into one of the more common patterns is not important. What *is* important is that your own process of self-assessment generates information that is useful to you. Nonetheless, I have identified the most common patterns, since they may be relevant for you or for the important people in your life.

- Men who value self-reliance and controlling their emotions. They prefer to keep their problems to themselves and may go to great lengths to do so. They are often unaware of the effect this has on their own well-being and their family.
- Women who value emotional expression and intimacy with loved ones. They may have male partners whose emotional lives are often hidden, and this can be a source of conflict and distance in the relationship.
- Women who were raised with a fairly traditional view of what it means to be a man. They are less comfortable around more emotionally expressive men and tend to behave in ways that discourage men from opening up more.
- Men who were raised with a fairly traditional view of what it means to be a man, and who also want to find ways to break free from some of the restrictions this has created for them. They may value emotional control and self-reliance, while wanting to find ways to share what is going on inside of them.

## SUMMARY

Self-assessment is a powerful process that can help you to understand the different roles men's silence and invisibility may be playing in your life. It is also a process that requires a good deal of sober self-honesty in order to be effective. When done well, it rarely results in yes/no answers to questions, and it should not be used as a way to figure out who is to blame for particular problems. Instead, the goal is to learn as much as you can about yourself or a particular man in your life. Some of the important areas to focus on include the degree to which hidden pain is an issue in your life, how you respond to this pain, what consequences this pain produces, your beliefs about what it means to be a man, and the personal values of greatest importance to you. Having a clear sense of each of these domains of life will put you in a much better position to make choices that work for you when you are faced with silent or invisible pain.

## PART II

BREAKING THE SILENCE AND
PROMOTING WELL-BEING

# Physical Well-Being

Guys will generally not seek medical treatment, for themselves or for others, except in certain clear-cut situations,
such as decapitation.

—DAVE BARRY[1]

Dave Barry's comment about men and medical treatment is satir-
ical, but it may not be far from the mark. Failure to attend to
men's physical well-being is one of the most tragic consequences
of invisible vulnerability in men's lives. In this chapter I consider
various ways that men's physical well-being is affected by silence
and invisibility. I then suggest a number of ways that both men
and women can relate to men's bodies in healthier ways that promote overall well-being.

## THE SILENT AND INVISIBLE BODY

On the face of it, it seems ludicrous to suggest that men's bodies
are silent or invisible. The fact is that compared to women, on
average men take up more physical space. Their voices are also

louder and their physical gestures more demonstrative. If you are not sure about this, just pay attention to body posture, voice tone, and nonverbal behavior the next time you are in a public setting with both men and women. Sitting in chairs, for example, men are more likely to slump back and extend their legs, while women are more likely to sit upright and keep themselves in a relatively contained space.

Men's bodies are also highly visible in the media. Consider how much televised air time is devoted to professional sports where broad shoulders, six-pack abs, and a host of statistics on men's bodies are front and center. ("He's six-six and 270; that's a hell of a lot of running back right there!") Popular science fiction and action films also portray men's bodies as physically imposing, often to the point of invincibility. Video games are similarly packed with suprahuman male characters whose muscular makeup from head to toe is highly salient in their overall presence.

Of course, the super-ripped, hypersexual, invincible man does not correspond to most *real* men in the world. Back on Earth, men's bodies are just as vulnerable and, in some ways, more vulnerable than women's. My colleague Will Courtenay (www.menshealth .org) has been a pioneer in raising awareness about the many problems that men face in their physical health. He has summarized several decades of research showing that, compared to women, men:

- Have higher mortality rates for all fifteen leading causes of death except Alzheimer's disease
- Die more than five years younger
- Account for 94 percent of all workplace fatalities
- Are less knowledgeable about their own health and take less responsibility for it

One of the most troubling findings is that men are far less likely than women to seek health care for *virtually all problems*, physical, mental, and anywhere in between. Over the long run, rugged self-reliance and dogged unwillingness to seek help can easily translate into a life cut short. Preventable testicular and prostate cancer are prime examples of how this particular version of silence and invisibility operates. Men's fear, shame, and embarrassment at testicular self-examination and undergoing a digital prostate exam are some of the major obstacles to engaging in routine preventative health care. That's probably not surprising. What is surprising is how difficult it can be to imagine living in a culture where most men would be comfortable talking about their testicles and their prostate glands with health care professionals. What is also surprising is that many (most?) men still get a case of the willies at even imagining such a situation, much less living it.

Personal, private, and public silence all play a role. Men themselves may be less likely to recognize that they have a health problem (personal silence), they may choose to keep it to themselves when they do recognize it (private silence), and they may be discouraged by their social network from talking openly about the problem (public silence). Research has shown that men's "health-risk behaviors," including keeping problems to themselves and not seeking medical care, play a major role in their reduced lifespan.[2] Studies also show that men ask fewer questions of their primary care physicians than do women, and physicians actually put fewer questions to male than to female patients.[3-5] The bottom line is that we are all involved in creating the pervasive silence and invisibility that surround men's physical health.

Many social scientists believe that these problems are largely a product of the ways we construct men's bodies in society. (*Construct* refers to the meanings, images, symbols, and ideologies we use to represent men's bodies.) These social processes are thought to shape how we feel about men's bodies, how we understand them, and how we choose to respond to them when problems arise.

Images abound that portray men's bodies as machines. From da Vinci's Vitruvian Man, through Charles Atlas, on to Arnold Schwarzenegger's portrayal of "the Terminator," and up to professional wrestling today, we love to see men's bodies as well-oiled, high-performance, ultrareliable pieces of machinery designed to accomplish tasks requiring physical strength, endurance, speed, agility, and invincibility. Of course, most men do not think of themselves as the Terminator. Nonetheless, we all cannot help but be influenced by these idealized, and largely dysfunctional, representations of the male body.

Men's bodies are frequently seen as objects to perform with rather than care for. In other words, the emphasis is on what men's bodies *should be able to do*, rather than *what they need*. The perfect male body is often represented as a machine designed for repeated peak performance, under even the most challenging of circumstances. Football players with outrageously painful, even life-threatening injuries who continue to play; ultimate fighters who physically dominate other men with few rules holding them back; gang members who are willing to kill or be killed for the sake of respect; frat boys who party all night and still hit the gym for power lifting by 7:00 a.m. The message is the same: the ideal male body is a performance machine. The more abuse it takes and bounces back, the more masculine it is. The more help it needs, the more you care for it and are concerned about it, the more feminine it (and by extension you) is/are.

So where does this leave the average man with regard to his own body? A good place to start is to ask what he learns about men's bodies growing up as a boy. All of the masculine norms I discussed in part I can affect how men think about their own bodies. Many men learn that their bodies should:

- be capable of marathon bouts of sexual performance
- always be up for sex
- be relatively immune to pain
- be able to recover from all injuries
- not need much sleep
- always be capable of lifting heavy objects
- require little to no medical care
- be able to digest any type and amount of food
- be able to process large quantities of alcohol

If this way of thinking about men's bodies strikes you as unhealthy, you're right. But it is certainly not outdated. You don't need to go much farther than the cover of magazines such as *Men's Health* to realize that performance (rather than health) is really what it's all about: work performance, athletic performance, and sexual performance.

Imagine how differently we might approach men's bodies if we thought of them as:

- needing regular rest
- benefiting from preventative health care
- capable of sensuality as well as sexuality
- vulnerable to life-threatening illnesses such as heart disease and cancer
- needing regular stretching to prevent muscle strain

We are also led to believe that a man's body is the purest measure of his masculinity. Being muscular is one way to use the body to demonstrate masculinity, but there are other ways as well. In fact, men who regularly abuse their bodies are often seen as highly masculine. Whether it is eating large quantities of high-calorie food, drinking too much alcohol, taking unnecessary physical risks, working insanely long hours, enduring intense pain, or sustaining a serious injury without seeking medical treatment, we are taught to see something heroically masculine in these actions.

## THOUGHTS ABOUT THE BODY

These cultural belief systems and ideologies shape the way both men and women think about men's bodies on a daily basis. There is bad news and good news here. The bad news is that by the time we are adults our thoughts about men's bodies are so ingrained that they can occur automatically and have a strong effect on our behavior. The good news is that it is possible to change our own thought processes. The first step is understanding how these thoughts and behaviors are related.

Over the last few decades psychologists have developed an understanding of how our thoughts influence us to feel and act in particular ways. In the most general sense, the process is as follows:

Event ———— Thoughts ———— Actions / Emotions

The acronym ETA is shorthand for the way events in your life, thoughts, and actions/emotions unfold. When events happen in our lives, the way we interpret their meaning influences how we subsequently feel and act. Let's take a simple example: Imagine that you arrive home one evening from work to find the front door open at a time when no one is supposed to be home. This event will lead to certain thoughts (*Is there a burglar in my house?* or *Maybe my kids are home early from their friend's house* or *I probably forgot to close the door this morning*). Depending on which of these thoughts pops into your head, you will be prone to have different reactions and different emotions. Thinking there is a burglar in your house is likely to prompt the emotion of fear and a response of calling the police. On the other hand, thinking that you left the door open may prompt a mild emotion of annoyance, and your behavior might include rolling your eyes and walking quickly inside.

This is a relatively straightforward example, but it illustrates a very powerful point: how we think about events that happen to us—day to day, hour to hour, moment to moment—has a powerful effect on how we act and feel. This is just as true when it comes to the nature of men's physical well-being as when it comes to burglars, open doors, and other events in our lives.

### Roy's Story

Injury and illness are areas where people's thoughts can have a particularly powerful effect on how they respond to a situation and how they feel about it. I am reminded of this whenever I think of a man with whom I had a very close relationship for many years. Roy was in his midseventies, and he had experienced a number of major medical illnesses in the previous five years, including heart disease and skin cancer. As if that were not enough, at the time he came to see me he had recently been diagnosed with Parkinson's disease.

Roy's attitude about his physical challenges was typically fairly calm and philosophical. It was not that he was in denial about his situation; in fact, he seemed quite realistic about it. He mentioned several times, for example, that he knew his type of Parkinson's disease was degenerative and that if it didn't kill him, it was certainly going to be a downhill progression in terms of quality of life. Nonetheless, Roy continued to read avidly, sculpt, paint, and enjoy other creative outlets, even as he struggled with his health virtually every waking hour of his life.

In the first couple of years that I knew Roy we worked on his adjustment to his illnesses. We made steady progress on reworking some of the thought processes that were preventing him from getting as much enjoyment out of life as he hoped to. The accompanying table presents some specific activities that were regularly difficult for Roy, the sorts of thoughts he was having that we wanted to change, and the new thoughts he came up with to help himself take a more healthy perspective on the situation.

| ROY'S THOUGHT PROCESSES | | |
|---|---|---|
| **Difficult Activity** | **Thoughts to Be Changed** | **New Thoughts** |
| Eating (because hands are trembling) | *What kind of life is this? I'm like an infant.* | *I'm not an infant. I'm a grown man in a challenging situation.* |
| Speaking (having trouble finding words to express an idea) | *I can't remember anything anymore, and I sound like an imbecile.* | *Actually, I remember most things. I don't sound nearly as strange to other people as I do to myself.* |
| Walking (losing balance and falling down) | *I can't trust my body anymore, so I might as well do nothing except sit in a chair.* | *It's true that I can't trust my body as well as I used to. But that doesn't mean I have to sit in a chair. I just need to be more careful.* |

In each case Roy was able to work on developing more adaptive ways to think about his situation, and the positive effect on his physical and mental well-being was noticeable. He began to spend more time outside. With the help of his wife, they made renovations to their home that allowed Roy to have more independence in his daily activities.

Meanwhile, Roy's Parkinson's disease continued to progress and eventually got to the point where he periodically lost control of his bladder. His doctor suggested wearing adult diapers, but Roy refused. Eventually, it got to the point where he would not leave the house for fear of having an accident. Roy also began to miss doctor's appointments. Over time, he became increasingly dependent on his wife, who loved him deeply and did whatever she could for him. Still, the extra pressure was getting to her, and Roy was aware that his increased level of dependence on her was adding substantial stress to their marriage.

When I asked Roy about the adult diaper he said, "I'm sorry. I just can't do that." I tried to dig deeper to understand the meanings that Roy attributed to wearing the diaper. At one point I said to Roy, "Don't get me wrong. I certainly understand not wanting to wear a diaper. It's a pain to do and definitely not an issue anyone would want to deal with. But what I want to understand is what it means to you about yourself if you were to wear one. I ask because it seems like this is about more than it being a hassle."

When I asked Roy this question I was asking him about his thought processes. I wanted to know what went through his mind when he thought about wearing one of the diapers. This was important because it was exactly those thoughts that got in the way of Roy leading a more rewarding life, even with his Parkinson's disease.

Roy understood that whatever he was thinking about wearing a diaper was not necessarily helping him. However, he had a hard time identifying his precise thoughts. That's not uncommon, particularly when such thoughts come from more deep-seated or long-standing beliefs. Sometimes it takes a little digging and some patience. Roy and I continued to discuss the issue for a couple of weeks until we finally had a breakthrough.

Roy's wife had found a bus service that would come and pick him up and take him shopping, to the doctor, or anywhere else he wanted to go. This would have been a huge step forward for them since Roy's wife didn't drive a car and his increasing tendency to stay housebound was leaving them both too isolated. Still, Roy refused to take the bus.

One day I asked him to imagine walking to the bus and stepping onto it. "What would be going through your mind in that moment?" I asked him. That question triggered the following interchange:

ROY: Well, I'd sure be hoping I didn't piss myself.

ME: Right, that would obviously be a drag if that happened. But that's what the diaper is for. Are you concerned that someone might see it happen?

ROY: Yeah, I think that's a big part of it. I don't want to sit there looking like a baby and stinking up the place.

ME: You don't want to look like a baby.

ROY: Right.

ME: Tell me what looking like a baby means.

ROY: Do I have to? [laughing]

ME: Well, yeah. Go for it. We're just doing a little investigating here, trying to find out why the diaper is such an issue.

ROY: OK. I guess I have this image of walking up to that bus, and there are a bunch of people already on it waiting to go somewhere and they're looking out the window at me. And here I come up with my baby diaper on. And I have to explain to the driver why I have this damn thing on. I have to tell him, "You know, I used to be able to walk by myself. I used to be a successful documentary filmmaker. But now I'm not any of that. Instead, I'm falling apart and I can't even control my own piss. So that's my story. And it's bad enough living it without having to show it to people."

I sat back in my chair, somewhat stunned by the graphic honesty of Roy's remarks. I was also struck by the variety of very powerful thoughts that Roy identified without even realizing it. These included:

*I'll have to explain myself.*
*I used to be successful, but now I'm not any of that.*
*I'm a baby if I wear this diaper.*
*I'm falling apart.*

Letting these various thoughts float in my own mind for a while, I tried to get a sense of what it really meant to Roy to face this next challenge in his illness. The word *pride* kept coming up for me. It was as if wearing this diaper was the final blow to Roy's sense of pride in his own independence and accomplishments, and to his sense of himself as a man. I asked Roy if thinking about putting on a diaper then led him to think, for example, *I'm no longer a man. I'm a child who is helpless, dependent, weak, and failing.* By the look on his face I could tell that this hit the mark squarely for Roy. He simply nodded.

I never suggested to Roy that he was wrong to think this way. Now that I understood what it was like for him, I could easily imagine myself having the same thoughts if I was in a similar situation. But at the same time, I couldn't believe that his way of thinking about the meaning of wearing a diaper was helping him. This is a crucial point: Focusing on your thinking about men's physical well-being is not about figuring out if you're right or wrong in the way you think. It is about determining whether or not the way you are thinking is helping you achieve your goals.

In Roy's case, he was ambivalent about leaving the house. On the one hand, he was understandably frightened about what might happen if he lost his balance or had another problem due to his Parkinson's symptoms. On the other hand, he was aware that his life was becoming more confined than he truly wanted it to be. So I put the question to him, "Is this way of thinking about things helping you get what you want out of life?" His response was honest, and I respected him for it. "I'm not sure," he said, "I need to think about it."

Unfortunately, that was the last time Roy and I talked. He died a couple of weeks later from a heart attack.

## HOW USEFUL IS YOUR THINKING?

Roy's story is a fairly dramatic example of a common situation: the way individuals think about men's physical well-being has a powerful effect on the way they behave and feel toward men. As I discussed in part 1, the consequences of not attending directly to men's physical well-being can be dramatic. It is therefore worth looking closely at your own thought processes and considering how helpful or harmful they are.

Let's start by considering some common situations involving challenges to a person's physical well-being. In each case, what thoughts might you have about yourself if you experienced the situation? If you are the partner of a man, imagine that he is the one facing each of these challenges and ask yourself what your own thoughts about his situation might be.

| *If this were to happen* | *I might think* |
| --- | --- |
| I developed an unexplained pain in my genital area | ? |
| I found out I had high blood pressure | ? |
| I began to worry about my drinking | ? |
| I developed repeated headaches | ? |
| I got pains in my stomach that would not go away | ? |

For many men, the pressure to experience and portray themselves as appropriately masculine can lead them to think about physical well-being in unproductive ways. I have known many men, for example, who had the following thoughts when they ran into a physical health problem:

*I don't want to make a big deal out of it.*

*This is embarrassing.*

*It will probably go away, so why worry about it?*

*Either it's going to kill me or it won't, so why worry about it?*

*I don't like to feel weak, so I'm not going to let this beat me.*

*I'm not the kind of guy who runs to the doctor every time he gets a little boo-boo.*

Some of these thoughts may be helpful under the right circumstances. There are definitely some advantages to adopting a fighting stance in the face of illness, for example. But others are largely unhelpful because they promote silence and invisibility. They are also driven by certain underlying *beliefs* about the body and how a man is supposed to act in the presence of threats to his physical well-being. Some of the more common beliefs men hold about their physical well-being include:

There is something "manly" about suffering through pain.

High levels of stress mean that I'm working hard and doing the right thing.

When my body breaks down it's my own fault.

There's something "gay" about worrying about my health.

Real men suck it up and move on.

I can't make a big deal out of this problem because people will think I can't handle it and I'm falling apart.

Now let's set these same beliefs alongside more adaptive ways of thinking (presented in italics).

- There is something "manly" about suffering through pain./ *Suffering doesn't make me a man. It takes courage to recognize that I have a health problem and to do something about it.*
- High levels of stress mean that I'm working hard and doing the right thing./*High levels of stress might mean that I'm overdoing it. Perhaps I need to think about how much stress I'm under and take better care of myself.*
- When my body breaks down it's my own fault./*It's not helpful to think this way. I may have done something to contribute to the problems I'm having, but feeling guilty or ashamed about it doesn't help.*

- There's something "gay" about worrying about my health./ *Everyone worries about their health on some level. My sexual orientation has nothing to do with it.*
- Real men suck it up and move on./*I can always choose to suck it up, or I can choose to do something about it.*
- I can't make a big deal out of this problem because people will think I can't handle it and I'm falling apart./*How do I know what other people will think? Plus, who cares what they think? If anything, they may think that I'm taking charge by addressing the problem directly.*

With a little practice you can pretty quickly learn to observe and challenge your own thought processes.

## MEN AND SEX

Men's true sexuality is typically one of the most silent and invisible aspects of their physical well-being. For that reason it is also poorly understood. One of the greatest myths, for example, is that men's sexual behavior is strictly caused by their biology. Although there are no doubt biological influences on human sexuality, men are also encouraged by powerful social norms and stereotypes to view their own sexuality in particular ways. When it comes to sex, society dictates that men should:

Want it all the time

Have multiple sexual partners

Be the dominant partner

Always perform or "satisfy" their partner as a sign of virility

Focus on physical gratification rather than emotional intimacy

Keep any problems or insecurities about sexuality to themselves

In contrast, most actual men do not conform to these stereotypes and societal expectations. When men feel secure in a trusting relationship, whether it's with a partner, a close friend, or a counselor, they are often able to share their questions, fears, and uncertainties about sexuality and sexual behavior. They may also reveal a greater desire for closeness and emotional intimacy, and less emphasis on "getting some," "being a stud," and so on. Research shows that men's partners are generally more satisfied in relationships when men are capable of greater emotional intimacy, sensitivity, and communication about sex.[6–7] One study found that the majority of men overestimate the importance of penis size to partners, and underestimate the size of their own penis compared to the average.[8–9] The bottom line is that the stereotype of the hypersexual marathon lover is not only inaccurate but also harmful to men's and women's physical and emotional well-being.

So why do so many men still buy into myths about their own sexuality? A large part of the problem is that men have internalized certain thought processes and behaviors surrounding sexuality that are a direct result of these larger societal stereotypes. Some of the most common and dysfunctional thoughts around sexuality include:

*Sex must always be amazing to be good.*

*Good sex always involves raging orgasms for my partner.*

*My success as a lover is measured by how often I have sex.*

*I should know what pleases my partner without having to ask.*

*If I'm not in the mood for sex, something must be wrong with me.*

*If I have problems "performing" sexually, it is very shameful.*

*I must have sex often to feel good about myself as a man.*

*My sex drive is uncontrollable because it's biologically based.*

*Birth control is a woman's responsibility (in heterosexual relationships).*

Again, let's compare these dysfunctional thoughts to more functional or helpful ways of thinking about men's sexuality.

- Sex must always be amazing to be good./*There are many different ways to enjoy sex. Sometimes it is more amazing than others, but it's unreasonable to expect it to be that way all of the time.*
- Good sex always involves raging orgasms for my partner./*People have orgasms in a variety of ways. Although orgasms feel good, they are not the only important part of sex. Closeness, fun, and humor are also enjoyable. It does not help me to judge myself by my partner's orgasms.*
- My success as a lover is measured by how often I have sex./*Sex is not a numbers game, and it's not a competition. How often I have sex is less important than whether both my partner and I are mutually satisfied with our sexual relationship.*
- I should know what pleases my partner without having to ask./*I can't read minds. There is nothing wrong with asking my partner what pleases him or her.*
- If I'm not in the mood for sex, something must be wrong with me./*It is normal to be more interested in sex sometimes than others. If I'm not interested, it doesn't mean there is anything wrong with me.*
- If I have problems "performing" sexually, it is very shameful./ *Most people have problems related to sexual performance at some*

*time in their lives. Getting down on myself about it doesn't help at all.*

- I must have sex often to feel good about myself as a man./*How often I have sex has nothing to do with how manly I am. Different men like to have different amounts of sex, and the same is true for women.*
- My sex drive is uncontrollable because it's biologically based./*Although the drive for sex in all human beings has a biological basis, this does not mean sexual behavior is uncontrollable. I am in charge of how I behave sexually.*
- Birth control is a woman's responsibility (in heterosexual relationships)./*Birth control is the responsibility of both partners in a relationship.*

## TALKING ABOUT PHYSICAL WELL-BEING AND MEN'S BODIES

One of the major challenges for those in relationships with silent and invisible men is finding ways to talk to them about problems. I will have much more to say about this in chapter 6 when we consider the effects of silence and invisibility in relationships. For now, it is worth considering different ways to talk to men about their bodies and their physical well-being. Some of the suggestions are based on good communication skills in general, while others have more to do with talking to men in particular.

Whenever a topic of conversation is potentially delicate it is very important to distinguish between (a) the issue you want to talk about, and (b) how you want to go about discussing it. The first is the *content* of the conversation, and the second is the *process* of the conversation. Oftentimes people never even reach the point of discussing the content because the process gets off track too quickly. For example, how often have you heard (or been part of) a conversation like this?

1ST PERSON: I'm worried about your health.

2ND PERSON: Oh great, not this again. I told you it's fine and I'm not going to the doctor.

1ST PERSON: OK. But why do you have to get so defensive about it?

2ND PERSON: I'm not defensive. I'm just telling you that I'm OK and I'm not going to the doctor.

1ST PERSON: It's the way you're saying it.

2ND PERSON: How am I saying it? I don't get this.

1ST PERSON: Like it's not even OK for me to say that I'm worried.

2ND PERSON: You can say whatever you want. But I'm not going to the doctor.

And so on . . .

Good communication is collaborative, respectful, and clear. Bad communication is often confrontational, polarized, and sometimes accusatory. When discussing men's physical well-being you need to do whatever you can to avoid getting into an argument, ending up on complete opposite sides of the issue, or criticizing the person you care about. This can be very difficult to achieve when emotions are running high.

I once worked with a married couple in which the man had been diagnosed with Guillain-Barré syndrome. (This is a very cruel disease in which the body's immune system attacks the nervous system. People suffering from it can have intermittent episodes of paralysis, and there is no known cure.) The feelings

ierated by his illness were so strong for both the husband and
e wife that they had a very difficult time discussing it without
ending up in an argument or simply unable to talk. They loved
each other very much and wanted to be there for each other.
However, the issues were just too overwhelming.

Even without a major threat to one partner's physical well-
being, most couples have trouble discussing issues related to men's
bodies and their physical well-being. Here are some suggestions
to get you on the right track toward effective communication. Note
that these suggestions are not foolproof, and some will work better with some men than others.

## RESPECT HIS DIFFICULTY IN TALKING

Many men are not used to having conversations in which they
find themselves emotionally vulnerable. In this regard, talking
about a physical problem would certainly qualify, particularly if a
man is not used to thinking of his body as a vulnerable part of
himself that needs to be cared for. Depending on the problem
(e.g., sexual dysfunction of some kind), talking about it might
also increase feelings of shame and embarrassment. A friend once
revealed to me that he and his wife had not had sex in several
years. Although they loved each other very much, and had a great
deal of emotional closeness in their relationship, his difficulties in
achieving and maintaining an erection were taking a toll on their
sexual relationship. My friend knew, of course, that I studied the
psychology of men, and we had spoken about men's sexuality on
numerous occasions. Still, it was too embarrassing a topic for him
to reveal to me personally. Even when he finally brought it up, the
conversation was open and shut very quickly.

Some men may also lack the vocabulary to talk about how

they feel about a problem, what their fears are, and so on. The point is not to avoid talking, but rather to recognize and respect that talking itself may be a difficult process. A man who seems to be stonewalling may simply be trying to avoid putting himself in an even more vulnerable situation; it's enough to have a problem with your physical health, but then to have to talk about it can add insult to injury. Sometimes simply acknowledging the difficulty ("I know you would rather not talk about this, and I appreciate the effort you are putting into it") is enough to keep the process on track.

## FIND A GOOD TIME AND PLACE TO TALK

Timing is everything. When one or both people are tired, stressed, or angry, it is almost never a good time to talk. Immediately upon returning home from work is also often a tough time. For some couples, simply finding a time when they are not occupied with children, work, or other responsibilities can be difficult. One useful approach is to schedule a time to talk. Let your partner know that you want to talk at some point soon, and that you realize now is probably not a good time. For some men, talking while engaging in a mutual activity, such as cooking, going for a walk, or going for a drive, is more comfortable than sitting and talking face-to-face.

## BE CONCISE

Many men are not used to having long, open-ended discussions about issues related to their well-being. Several years ago I spent a year working on a spinal cord injury unit. Not surprisingly, the majority of patients were men. (Men are far more likely than women to suffer spinal cord injuries, largely because they engage more frequently in risk-taking behaviors.) In addition to their obvious life upheavals, both physically and emotionally, many of the men I spoke with were also struggling to find ways to talk (or not talk) with loved ones about their injuries and their new lives. Although most of them wanted to talk, many of the men were initially uneasy with the process, particularly when it was open-ended. They needed to know that they would not be "stuck" talking at length and running the risk of being overwhelmed by emotions they were not prepared to control.

Try to keep initial conversations short and to the point so he knows there's an "out." You might want to schedule a fixed period of time (say, ten to fifteen minutes) for your initial conversation. You can always schedule additional time. And if it turns into a longer, more open conversation, that's an added benefit. This is far preferable to expecting a single long conversation and then being disappointed that it didn't go the way you wanted it to.

## BE DIRECT AND FRANK

If you're worried, tell him so. If you're afraid, tell him that too. If you're not sure how to start talking, start there. ("I want to talk to you, but I don't know how to start. Please let me stumble a bit until I figure out how to say what I want to say.") Many men respect directness in communication because it fits with their pragmatic orientation toward getting things done rather than wallowing in uncertainty. As an example, imagine wanting to talk to a man about a pain he's been experiencing in his testicles and hoping that you can encourage him to see the doctor. Now compare these three different approaches to starting a conversation:

1. I want to talk to you about that thing that's been going on.
2. How have you been feeling lately? Any change?
3. I want to talk to you about the pain you have in your testicles. It is worrying me.

The third statement is frank and direct, while the first two beat around the bush.

## OWN YOUR OWN FEELINGS

If you're worried about his well-being, own your own worry. This means not assuming that he should be worried, or trying to argue him into viewing his situation differently. If his reluctance to talk to you hurts your feelings, say so. But don't assume that your feelings are the result of his deliberate attempts to hurt you. The bottom line is that however you feel around a man who is silent and invisible with regard to his physical well-being, it's exactly that: how *you* feel. Recognizing this should help you to acknowledge and respect your own feelings. For example, just because he is keeping a stiff upper lip about a medical condition doesn't mean that you're supposed to do the same thing. It should also help you to avoid trying to make him responsible for how you feel, a process that almost universally leads to defensiveness. If his silence and invisibility are threatening to you, this does not mean that he is the cause of those feelings.

## AVOID ANGER IF AT ALL POSSIBLE

Anger is a natural human emotion, and there is nothing inherently wrong with it. However, when the goal is to engage in a conversation about a difficult topic that is not usually discussed, anger can be very destructive and it can shut the process down quickly. Some men are extremely sensitive to criticism and will interpret anger as an indication that they have done something wrong. It is not that your anger is wrong or unjustifiable. You may have every right to be angry. What I want to raise your awareness of is the degree to which anger is helping or hindering you when you're trying to have a productive conversation.

It also helps to recognize that anger is often what psychologists call a secondary emotion; it is a response to other more vulnerable emotions such as anxiety, fear, and sadness. If these emotions are too threatening to experience at the time, you may find that you or the man you are talking to begin to express anger as a way of avoiding or trying to take control of the more painful feelings. If you recognize this response in yourself, you can label it just that way by saying something like: "I realize that I'm getting angry about this. It's because I'm scared/afraid/sad, and I'm worried that things are not going to be all right. Can we start over and try to get back on track?"

For all of these reasons it is typically best to avoid angry communication, at least during your first few forays into discussing a sensitive issue. If anger about the issue is a major part of what you need to discuss, it will come up. When it does, try to take it slow and follow the other suggestions for effective communication when anger is on the table.

## KNOW WHAT CONTENT YOU WANT TO COVER AND HAVE SOME GOALS IN MIND

It is very helpful to know what you want to accomplish when you enter into a conversation with a man about aspects of his body.

Do you want to influence him in some way? Do you want to share your feelings? Do you want to better understand his? Do you want to find out how he is doing? Knowing what you want to accomplish is key to staying on track. If you have had similar conversations in the past and they tend to get off track, try to figure out at what point they go awry. Is it when he gets defensive? Is it when you get angry? Figure out an alternative approach to take when these moments arise, and try it out. It may help to role-play it in advance with a friend.

## IMAGINE BEING HIM

Many men behave in ways that can ward off other people's attempts to care for them (saying "I'm fine," "I don't want to talk about it," "You're making a big deal out of this"). But this does *not* mean that they don't want to be understood. It simply means that they are uncomfortable being in a vulnerable position. For those who care about them, this resistance to being vulnerable can be extremely off-putting. Nonetheless, empathy (rather than sympathy) is a key to effective communication. The more you can understand what it's like to have a problem, to not want to worry about it, to fear talking about it, and to prefer to ignore it, the more you can empathize with his situation.

## PROMOTING HEALTH AND PHYSICAL WELL-BEING

As I have suggested throughout this chapter, men are under substantial pressure to deny their physical vulnerabilities and instead to present their bodies as if they are invincible self-regulating machines always ready to perform. Changing the way you think about the male body is one way to combat these harmful distortions of reality. Another way is to directly change your behavior with regard to physical health and well-being. Changing how you talk to men is one way I have already covered. If you are a man, there are also direct behavioral changes that you can make. These include:

- Exercising regularly
- Relaxing regularly
- Eating a healthy diet
- Being honest with a partner about your feelings regarding your sexuality and your sex life
- Reducing stress
- Performing regular testicular self-examinations
- Having regular checkups with your physician
- Following through on medical advice
- Getting adequate sleep
- Decreasing risky behavior
- Increasing safety precautions when appropriate

## SUMMARY

While we often idolize men whose bodies are tall, muscular, athletic, and seemingly immune to pain, we also turn a blind eye and a deaf ear to the realities of men's vulnerabilities when it comes to their physical well-being. This is particularly true in the areas of injury, illness, and sexuality. Paying attention to the thoughts and beliefs you have about men's physical well-being can help you to bring about positive change in your life and a more realistic perspective. The facts are:

- Challenges to men's physical well-being are more the norm than the exception.

- Men do experience worries and concerns about their bodies.
- Many men can and do want to discuss their concerns, but they must overcome significant obstacles to doing so.
- There are numerous myths about men's sexuality that constrain both men and women and often prevent development of honest and satisfying sexual relationships.
- Most men desire emotional intimacy as well as sexual gratification, although society often encourages them to focus more on the latter than the former.

In addition to recognizing the realities about men's physical well-being, there are behavioral changes you can make in the way you talk to men about their bodies. These include getting the timing right, being direct and concise, respecting men's difficulties in talking about certain topics, having goals for the conversation in mind, and setting time limits on initial conversations. There are several health-promoting behaviors that men can engage in, including paying attention to diet, getting regular physical exercise, learning to relax regularly, having annual checkups, performing self-examinations, and reducing stress as much as possible.

## · 5 ·

# Emotional Well-Being

Like many people in the field of psychology, I am not particularly fond of telling people what I do for a living. It is an inside joke in the profession because when most of us say, "I'm a psychologist," we hear the same reactions: "Are you analyzing me right now?"; "You must have had an unhappy childhood"; "I'd better watch what I say around you"; and so on. Over the years I thought I had heard all the possible responses, but when I started studying men's mental health things got ramped up a notch. Some people are so stunned that they have no idea how to respond. Others make jokes: "*What* mental health?"; "Boy, have I got a case for you!" And then there's the look that says, "Why are you doing this? Can't you leave well enough alone? There's nothing to study here." I believe these reactions reflect the fact that taking an interest in men's mental health is like hitting a cultural nerve; it causes people to twitch uncomfortably. As one of my colleagues recently said, "When I think about men and mental health the first thing that comes to mind is, *Don't go there*."

This chapter is all about going there. We will explore a wide range of issues related to how men experience, express, and respond to issues of mental health and other problems in living. The chapter is not just about mental health in the traditional sense of mental disorders. Many people, both men and women, struggle with very powerful issues related to their emotional well-being that, for a variety of different reasons, do not qualify as a mental illness. The question of whether mental illness is truly distinct from normal human functioning, or whether all human functioning exists on a continuum, is a hotly debated issue by professionals in this field.

I take the position that mental health disorders are very real problems that require compassionate and effective care. I also believe that limiting our understanding of men's emotional well-being to diagnosable mental illnesses would be a serious mistake. Many men are more than ready to minimize and disregard stress, the blues, hassles, "everyday life," and so on, as inevitable parts of living. In other words, why make a big deal out of it? One of my goals in this chapter is to show you how men's desire to not make a big deal out of things powerfully affects their overall well-being, regardless of whether problems rise to the level of a mental disorder. Research has shown that high levels of work stress, relationship conflict, anger, stressful life events, and other nondisorders have profound effects on our overall emotional well-being.[1-4] How we approach these issues in our life is as or more important than the fact that they exist. Thus, in order to appreciate how silence and invisibility operate in men's emotional well-being, it is necessary to examine how men relate to emotional experiences in general. For all of these reasons, when I speak of *mental health* I am referring to overall human emotional well-being rather than the more limited category of diagnosable *mental disorders*.

## MEN, MASCULINITY, AND MENTAL HEALTH

When I talk with the public about these issues I often begin by saying that, in most cultures, men and mental health go together about as well as orange juice and toothpaste; something about the combination just doesn't leave a good taste in our mouths. The very *idea* of masculinity and mental health seems like an unnatural mixture for most people. Historically, mental health problems were thought of as personal weaknesses or failures of character, as opposed to real problems with real causes that require effective treatment. In contrast, we think of masculinity as involving toughness, stoicism, and control over one's weaknesses. In short, the stereotype is that there's nothing very manly about suffering from depression, anxiety, bipolar disorder, or other mental health problems. For this reason, mental health was also thought of historically as a "woman's problem." In fact, women are more often diagnosed with mental health problems than are men. But as you might suspect, this is *far from definitive proof* that women are actually more likely to suffer from mental health problems. First, there are no clear-cut biological markers for the overwhelming majority of mental illnesses. Instead, we diagnose them by the presence or absence of symptoms that are predominantly behavioral rather than biological (crying, worrying, sleeping too much, sleeping too little, and so on).

It is not hard to see that our assumptions and preconceptions about what is normal or abnormal behavior could play a major role in what mental illnesses we are ready to see as a culture. If we assumed that men's behavior is the standard by which other abnormal behavior should be judged, we would pretty quickly come to the conclusion that women suffer more mental illness than men, simply because we are better prepared to see problems in women's behavior than in men's. On the other hand, if women's behavior was seen as the norm and men's as the exception, we would probably be more ready to diagnose mental health problems in men.

To get a better sense of this, have a look at the following phrases. Read them to yourself, and after each one ask yourself whether it seems like it might be a symptom of mental illness or "psychological problems" more generally.

| | |
|---|---|
| Crying a lot | Being unable to cry |
| Worrying a lot | Never allowing yourself to worry |
| Needing other people to feel good | Not needing other people |
| Excessively low self-esteem | Excessively high self-esteem |
| Purposely injuring yourself | Purposely injuring someone else |

If you are like most people, you are more likely to see the behaviors and feelings listed in the left-hand column as indicators of an underlying mental health problem. It also turns out that these "symptoms" are seen by most people as more stereotypically feminine, whereas the ones in the right-hand column are seen as more masculine. Because we are more prepared to see stereotypically feminine behaviors as problems, we are more prepared to see women as suffering from psychological disorders than men. If we assumed, for example, that the inability to cry, refusal to worry about anything, and an excessively high opinion of oneself were markers of an underlying disorder (perhaps "Grandiose Emotional Restriction Disorder," or "GERD" for short), we might see higher rates of mental illness in men.

In short, the statistically higher prevalence of many mental health problems in women does not necessarily mean that women have more mental health problems than men. Consider the following:

- Although men are half as likely as women to be diagnosed with depression, they are four times more likely to take their own lives.
- Men outnumber women in rates of drug and alcohol abuse approximately two to one.
- The vast majority of violent crimes are committed by men, and a large proportion of incarcerated men meet criteria for a diagnosable psychiatric illness.

## THE PARADOX OF MEN'S EMOTIONAL WELL-BEING

The first step to enhancing your understanding of men's mental health is beginning to wrestle with one of the great paradoxes of gender: On the one hand, the overwhelming majority of scientific evidence suggests that men and women are far more similar than they are different when it comes to psychological characteristics, emotions, intelligence, relationships, and so on.[5] On the other hand, our common sense and everyday experience appear to tell us otherwise; it *seems* that men and women are just plain different. This perception of difference is not limited to the area of emotional well-being. We are told that women are more right-brained, men are more left-brained; women like to share, men like to keep things to themselves; women like art, men like science; and so on. For a variety of reasons, as a society we are particularly prone to generalize about differences between men and women with regard to psychological processes. Consider how often you have heard the following:

Women get sad; men get angry.

Men don't ask for help when they have problems, and women do.

Women like going to therapy; men won't touch it with a ten-foot pole.

Women want to talk about how they feel; men want to solve the problem.

Let's look at some of these pieces of conventional wisdom in greater detail and see what scientific research has to say about them. First, studies do tend to show that *on average* men are more likely than women to express anger, and women are more likely to express sadness.[6] However, these are *average* differences between samples of men and women. Many women express anger, and many men express sadness, depending on the situation. Consider how common it is for male athletes to shed tears following a huge win or loss. And we have all seen women express anger when they are frustrated about something or have been treated unfairly. Just because there is an *average* difference between two groups does not mean that that difference is a particularly *large* one. Nor does it mean that every *individual* in a group follows the group *pattern*.[7]

There are also small average differences between the genders, combined with tremendous variability within each gender, with regard to help-seeking behavior, identifying emotions, and sharing problems with others. With few exceptions, men are not really that different than women when it comes to their mental health. And yet as a society we expect them to be. This paradox sets into motion powerful social processes that influence how men experience, express, and respond to problems in their lives. It works like this:

- As a society we dramatically exaggerate differences between men and women when we see them or want to see them. As a result:
- There is an *expectation* that men *should be* different from women. So:
- Many men fear that they might be perceived as feminine if they behave in ways that are not considered appropriate for their gender.
- Ultimately, the fear of difference *partly* creates the reality of difference.

## THE POWER OF POLARIZING LENSES

One of the most important ideas to take from this paradox is that our perception of gender has a tremendously powerful effect on how it plays out in our lives. Sandra Bem, a leading researcher in the psychological study of gender, compares gender to a lens that shapes our perceptions of men's and women's behavior, and sorts these perceptions into what we view as appropriately male/female and masculine/feminine. At various points in her book *The Lenses of Gender*, Bem refers to the polarizing effects of gendered lenses. This metaphor of a polarized lens strikes me as an extremely accurate way of describing some of the most powerful influences on the silence and invisibility that surround men's emotional well-being.[8]

Polarizing lenses sort incoming information into discrete categories. In the case of a *physically* polarizing lens, which you might find on a pair of sunglasses, light is filtered in such a way that all waves at a ninety-degree angle from the direction you are looking are removed. Gender is seen through a *socially* polarizing lens. This metaphorical lens comes into our vision at various times and shapes what we see, how we feel about it, and, at times, what we choose to do or not do. It is a polarizing lens because it frames things in very oppositional ways: right/wrong, OK/not OK, black/white, male/female, and so on.

Polarizing lenses are important because they have the subtle but powerful effect of leading us to see some things more clearly by filtering out others. As a result, the world seems simpler and more clearly defined, regardless of whether it actually works that way. Whether this is helpful or harmful depends on the situation. Physically polarizing lenses, for example, help us to see bluer skies and less glare in our vision. Socially polarizing lenses can help us make quick decisions about what we think is right or wrong, masculine or feminine, and so on. But they can also severely distort what we see and limit our options for effectively coping with situations when things don't neatly line up into discrete categories.[9] For example, the tendency to think in black-and-white terms is common in people suffering from clinical depression. Seeing gender through a polarizing lens is itself a form of black-and-white thinking.

Polarizing lenses are so common that we often forget we are looking through them. They exert their effects on our perceptions of numerous issues in our lives, from the most mundane to the most profound. Let me tell you a story from my own life that illustrates just how quickly polarizing lenses can come to complicate a seemingly insignificant decision.

## THE CHALLENGE OF BUYING A PIPE

My father smoked a pipe when I was growing up, and I have always had positive associations with the look of briar pipes and the smell of burning tobacco. About a year ago I decided to try smoking a pipe and borrowed one from a friend. I quickly found out that I enjoyed this activity, so I decided to buy a pipe of my own. I visited the local tobacconist in town, and when I asked him to help me select a pipe, we had the following conversation:

TOBACCONIST:  Straight or bent?

ME:  I'm sorry . . . ?

TOBACCONIST:  Do you want a straight or a bent stem?

ME:  I don't know. I guess I never thought about it.

TOBACCONIST:  Well, that's the first decision you have to make.

ME:  How do you make a decision like that? I mean, whether I'm going to smoke a straight or a bent pipe.

TOBACCONIST:  I don't know. It's a personal preference. Different styles. Are you more like Sherlock Holmes (bent) or Cary Grant (straight)?

ME:  Umm. . . . I have to think about that.

As I sat there and wondered whether I was more like a fictional British private investigator or an ultracool handsome movie star from days past, I wasn't sure how to proceed. "Are you sure straight and bent are the only options?" I asked. "Yep," he replied, "that's the way it works." So I bought a pipe with a bent stem, figuring I wasn't quite ready to venture into Cary Grant territory.

As I left the store my psychologist brain started working. First, you didn't have to be a Freudian to grasp the significance of *straight* versus *bent* for a psychology of men. The immediate impact of the word *straight* for many men is going to be more loaded than 95 percent of words in the English language, simply by virtue of its powerful associations with two of the dominant masculine norms I described in part I: heterosexuality and sexual prowess. By the time most men reach the age of eighteen they have more than learned the rules "be straight" (don't be gay), "be straight" (keep it up no matter what), and "be straight" (stand in line and don't deviate).

You might argue that straight/bent is simply a convention that facilitates selling pipes. But if that's true, how do we account for the immediately intuitive distinction between bent (nerdy, intellectual private detective masculinity) and straight (handsome Casanova lover masculinity)? The bottom line is that straight/bent is a conveniently gendered polarizing lens that can take something as simple as the type of pipe you smoke and load it with psychological significance. The last thing that struck me was how powerful polarizing lenses must be if they can creep into something as seemingly trivial as pipe selection. How powerful could they be when the stakes were higher?

### Jerry's Story

My first hint of the potential power of polarizing lenses in men's emotional well-being came early on in our research into men with symptoms of depression who preferred not to seek treatment. I interviewed a man named Jerry who appeared to be suffering from a classic case of clinical depression. Jerry was a fifty-five-year-old man who told me that for the past several years he had been regularly experiencing difficulty sleeping, trouble concentrating, feeling down or blue, and being a lot more irritable. All of my training led me to see Jerry's situation through a lens of "depression."

But Jerry did not see it this way at all. From his perspective, depression was a mental illness, and he most certainly was *not* dealing with that problem. In his own words: "As long as I can still get out of bed and go to work, I don't think I am depressed. Being depressed would be like, I don't know, the ultimate failure in being able to handle things. I can still handle things, so I don't think I am depressed."

I asked Jerry what he would call his situation. He shrugged and said, "I don't know. I guess it's just life. I've seen depression. My wife has it, and that's just not me. She can't hold it together, and so I guess she needs medication. I haven't fallen apart yet, so I guess I'm still OK at this point."

Jerry saw his emotional life through a polarizing lens. There were only two possibilities: the mental illness of depression and ". . . just life." Reading a little further into his comments, I wondered if Jerry viewed depression as a feminine problem rather than a masculine one ("My wife has it").

Jerry also seemed to be sorting human problems into two categories of severity: a total breakdown in functioning versus "normal unhappiness." Although there are certainly differences in severity between clinical levels of depression and periodic unhappiness, Jerry was experiencing some pretty major problems in his life (chronic irritability, trouble concentrating, sleep problems, and blue moods). I was struck by his complete lack of awareness that being unhappy on a regular basis was a problem. It was as if he was saying, "How things are on the inside for me is pretty much irrelevant. What matters is how I am doing on the outside. As long as I can fulfill my duties, particularly at work, everything is pretty much fine." In other words, there are only two possibilities: If you experience a complete breakdown in functioning, you may have a mental illness called depression. Otherwise, you don't have a problem, you don't need help, and your best bet is to keep quiet about it and keep moving forward in life.

Jerry's story illustrates some of the problems of seeing emotional well-being through a polarizing lens. Jerry's need to see his emotions as normal versus abnormal made it very difficult for him to take his own inner pain seriously. It was as if he saw a world where there are only two types of problems: those serious enough to be called real illnesses, and those that require you to suck it up and move on. Because he could not tolerate seeing himself in the former camp, he inevitably ended up in the latter. Jerry's polarizing lens also severely limited how he could cope with his situation. He categorically ruled out seeing a counselor since, in his eyes, therapy was only for mental health problems and he did not have one of those. He saw himself as the only one who could do anything to help his situation. Because he had tried to make a difference in how he felt, and was not successful, he concluded that his only option at this point was to suffer in silence.

## MORE POLARITIES

Polarizing lenses can create several other artificial oppositions that have equally restrictive effects. These include:

weak/strong
in control/out of control
self-reliance/dependency
mental/physical

Many men who are struggling with emotional pain in their lives are trapped into viewing it through one or more of these polarities. It makes sense that the tendency to sort experiences into these sorts of categories is driven by the gender paradox I described earlier. In each case, one half of the polarity tends to be seen as more feminine and the other half as more masculine. Because men are taught from a very young age to avoid being seen by others (and thus to avoid seeing oneself) as feminine, they are often not only trapped in a polarized view but also restricted to living out only one side of the opposition.

Imagine, for example, that a man loses his job due to an economic recession. Research has shown that, along with divorce and the death of a loved one, the loss of a job is one of the most stressful life events that can put people at risk for mental health problems such as depression.[10–11] Ideally, under such circumstances a person would be able to: (a) recognize that he or she is experiencing a problem, (b) communicate it to others who might be able to help or at the very least empathize, and (c) seek professional help if it is warranted.

Imagine now that this man sees both the experience of depression and seeking professional help as weak and gutting it out on your own as strong. He may also view seeking professional help (either counseling or medication) as an example of giving up control and being dependent. It's not hard to see how such a person could quickly equate both being depressed and getting help as essentially feminine and adamantly avoid both acknowledging the depression and seeking treatment.

Am I saying that the root of all men's problems is the fear of being perceived as feminine? I would not go that far. In fact, as far as we can tell from the available evidence, the actual causes of depression, despair, loneliness, isolation, anxiety, and so on, are largely the same in men as in women.[12] Where the gender paradox and polarizing lenses come into play is in how men *respond to problems in their lives once they emerge*.[13] To feel sad is universally human. But what a man makes of that experience, how he expresses it, and what he chooses to do (or not do) about it is strongly affected by the way he perceives it.

## TAKING OFF THE SUNGLASSES

Once you are more aware of the power of polarizing lenses in shaping your perception of men's emotional well-being, you can decide whether you want to take them off or leave them on. Getting to this point of self-awareness and change requires vigilance and some practice since polarizing lenses often make things seem so natural that it is easy to forget that you have them on.

The first step is to identify when and where polarizing lenses are affecting your perceptions. The following exercise is helpful in this regard. Read the four statements below, which present different ways of viewing your own emotions. Then consider how much you agree with each one (not at all, somewhat, very much). Do your best to answer honestly in terms of how you *usually* think about things, rather than how you think you *should*.

- *Either I'm weak enough to let my emotions gain control of me, or I'm strong enough to master them myself.*
- *Either I stay in control of my situation, or I lose control.*
- *Either I handle my problems on my own, or I'm dependent on others for solutions.*
- *Either my problems have a real physical basis to them, or they're all in my head.*

As you could probably tell, each of these statements is phrased in terms of different polarities (weak/strong, in control/out of control, self-reliance/dependence, mental/physical). Agreeing with one or more of these statements may indicate that you tend to view emotional difficulties through a polarizing lens. This may apply not only to your own emotional difficulties but also to those of others.

## DAVID'S PANIC ATTACKS

I once interviewed a twenty-five-year-old man, David, who suffered from regular unexpected panic attacks. If you have ever had a panic attack, you know how terrifying and uncomfortable they can be. If you haven't had one, imagine what your body and mind would do in a span of five seconds if you saw a grizzly bear charging toward you; now imagine that your body and your mind did the same thing multiple times a week, for five to ten minutes at a time, out of the blue, when no grizzly bears or other real threats were anywhere to be found. When people have repeated panic attacks that occur for no reason, they can easily develop a form of psychiatric disorder in which they will go to great lengths to avoid having attacks, including, in the most severe cases, never leaving the house.

David had been suffering from panic attacks for six months when I interviewed him, and one of the first things I asked him was whether he had tried to get help. "Are you kidding?!" he replied. "I was at my doctor's office the next morning the first time this happened, and I've been back once a month ever since. He gave me some medication which sort of helps, but not that much. Still, I go to see him regularly because I definitely need help with this."

I then asked David if he had considered therapy or counseling. His response surprised me:

DAVID: Why would I need counseling?

ME: Perhaps to help with the panic attacks?

DAVID: How would that help? The panic attacks are a physical thing. My doctor said they're caused by my nervous system being sort of tweaked. It turns on when it's not supposed to and has a hard time turning off, is what he told me.

ME: Well, there's definitely some truth to that. But many people think, and there's actually a lot of scientific evidence to support this, that your own thoughts and behaviors can also contribute to panic.

DAVID: I've seen that happen sometimes, like when I'm really stressed I'm more likely to have an attack. But therapy is for people whose problems are in their head, right?

ME: Well, it's not really that simple. What's in our heads affects our bodies and vice versa. So, many times it helps to work on what's in your head as well as what's going on physically in your body.

DAVID: I don't know about that. I think my girlfriend would never let me hear the end of it if she found out I was going to counseling. It would be an "I told you so" fest for weeks because she's been saying all along that this is all in my head.

Although I was not doing therapy with David, I couldn't resist the temptation of pointing out the degree to which he was looking at his situation in an artificially polarized way. The truth is that problems like anxiety and depression are neither "all in your head" nor "all in your nervous system in your body." The mind and the body are intimately linked, so much so that many scientists now view the distinction as arbitrary and not particularly useful. Plus research has shown that panic disorder can be effectively treated with the right form of counseling in as few as six to eight sessions.[14–15]

Unfortunately, David's polarizing lens was restricting him from taking full advantage of the options available to him. To

make matters worse, he appeared to be in a relationship with someone who took a similarly polarized view of his situation.

If David had been able to take off his polarizing lenses, he
would have begun to see his situation in much more helpful
shades of gray. His panic attacks, for example, were neither solely
in his head nor limited to his nervous system. David would have
begun to understand that he could have a direct effect on how his
body responded to anxiety by changing how he thought about his
situation. And the reverse was true as well: the more David could
do to take care of himself physically, the better off he would be
mentally and emotionally. David's partner also had much to gain
by seeing shades of gray; her continued insistence that his problems were all in his head was adding fuel to David's resistance to
seeking effective treatment.

## BOB CHANGES HIS PRIORITIES

Sometimes it takes a particularly meaningful set of experiences to
help people realize that they have been seeing the world in polarities. I was recently at a party and overheard a very moving story to
this effect. A man named Bob, in his early sixties, was standing
next to his grown daughter and explaining to a group of friends
that many years ago he had shifted his priorities from work to family in a way that produced lasting positive effects on his relationships. Bob's daughter nodded the whole time as he described the
years when she was a young child: he was in the military and also
working a part-time job in order to make ends meet. In his mind
there was no other option but to work upwards of eighty hours a
week in order to put food on the table.

"That's my job in the family. That's what I thought to myself,"
Bob said. Although he did not state it directly, it seemed clear that

"because I'm a man" was part of that thought process. The result of all this work was that he rarely saw his wife or young children.

One evening while Bob was working late at his second job, the song "Cat's in the Cradle" came on the radio. This well-known folk song by Harry Chapin tells the story of a man with a grown son who is looking back on how absent he was during his son's development. The narrator now desires greater closeness with his son. However, in the final verse of the song he realizes, ". . . my boy was just like me"; his son is so busy with work that he has no time for a deeper relationship with his father. When Bob heard this song in the early 1970s, it hit him like a lightning bolt. He quickly quit his second job and began to spend more time with his family, a change that produced lifelong positive effects in his and his family's quality of life.

## QUESTIONS TO HEIGHTEN YOUR AWARENESS

An eye-opening experience triggered by a particular song, book, or movie, or a set of real-life events, can help a person realize when polarized vision is keeping his or her emotional life hidden. But waiting around for such meaningful experiences is only one way to go about changing your perspective. You can also do it by intentionally heightening your awareness of the lenses through which you see your life. When you become aware that you are less happy, less satisfied, or generally discontent emotionally, it can be very helpful to regularly ask yourself the following questions: Am I seeing certain situations in polarities? If so, is this restricting the options I am allowing myself in order to cope effectively with the situations I'm in?

If it seems like things are just unavoidably black and white, consider the following questions:

- Is there a way that both perspectives can be true rather than having to be one or the other?
- What middle grounds exist?
- Are things really this black and white?

Few things in the world are black and white, except perhaps life and death, and even that distinction is questionable at a purely biological level!

## HOW MEN ARE ABLE TO HIDE IN PLAIN SIGHT

Unfortunately, many of us view men's hidden pain as normal. So when a man is able to open up and share his vulnerability, we treat him as the exception rather than the rule. Our culture is full of messages that boys will be boys, men will be men, and "talking about feelings" is a woman's thing. But just because something is common does not mean that it is natural. Nor does it mean that it is intended to be that way, or that it is healthy.

It is as if we've all been brainwashed to think that men's inner lives *should* be silent and invisible. When a male family member rarely smiles and spends most of his time sitting in front of the television, we call him "Grumpy Uncle Charley" and let him be. When a teenage boy starts sleeping late every morning, stays away from his friends, and mumbles, "I'm fine, it's no big deal," we tell ourselves that he is going through a phase. When a man loses his job, starts drinking more alcohol, and says angrily that he doesn't want to talk about it, we "give him his space."

These examples all illustrate one of the biggest obstacles to making men's emotional lives more visible. We have become so accustomed to ignoring outward expressions of what is going on inside of men that *we can't register the fact that we are unable to see and hear what is happening with men.* As a result, many men's true inner lives are hiding in plain sight; visible if we choose to look closely, but rendered invisible because of the polarizing lenses most of us have been taught to look through. This combination of some men's tendency to hide vulnerability through the expression of more masculine emotions, and society's readiness to treat those emotions as normative for men, results in a number of common scenarios. In the following paragraphs I describe these scenarios in terms of different characters whose hidden pain is often seen as normal.

## GRUMPY UNCLE CHARLEY

Everyone has known a Grumpy Uncle Charley. He rarely smiles at family get togethers. Instead he sits in his favorite chair quietly watching the television, and perhaps drinking beer, wine, or a cup of coffee. Everyone accepts his presence and knows not to bother him. If a young child asks, "What's wrong with Uncle Charley? How come he never smiles and he's always sitting in that chair?" the response is, "That's just the way he is. He's always been like that."

When I describe Grumpy Uncle Charley to students or members of the public, heads begin to nod without fail. There is something very familiar and almost iconic about this presentation of men's emotional distress. Still, most of us are much more familiar with its outward presentation (grumpiness) than we are with the pain underneath. This is why I will often ask people to imagine what it's like to be Uncle Charley. You might literally try this at your next family get-together, or you can imagine what it would be like to do the following things: Don't talk much, if at all. Sit or stand off to the side, perhaps watching the television. Do not smile and do not laugh. Try this for at least ten minutes and notice what happens inside you and around you.

Many people report that they had expected to feel very angry and were surprised by how sad and alone they actually felt. There is clearly a difference between what they projected on the outside and what was actually going on underneath. People also report that others quickly asked, "Is something wrong?"

On the one hand, this is not surprising, since most people who try this experiment do it to see what it is like to behave *differently* than they normally do. Because their behavior stands out to others, those people are naturally concerned. Yet this still begs the question: why aren't people concerned and asking Uncle Charley if anything is wrong? You might say the reason is that when Uncle Charley behaves in this way there's nothing unusual about it. That is precisely the point. Despite the fact that Uncle Charley might be in a tremendous amount of emotional pain, we see his behavior as normal. His inner vulnerability is hiding in plain sight.

## SOLEMN SAM

Many parents of adolescent boys are familiar with Solemn Sam. Sam doesn't get too emotional about anything, and cool is the name of his game. When he walks he shuffles awkwardly with his arms hanging down, his eyes staring blankly at the ground. If you address him, he is more likely to nod or mutter than to look you in the eye. If you ask him how things are going, he'll tell you with one word: "Fine." Still, he leaves you feeling uneasy at times because there seems to be so much more below the surface. On the other hand, you've often been told, "That's just the way teenage boys are. He'll grow out of it."

## POSITIVE PETE

If you ask Positive Pete how he's doing, there's only one answer: "Great!" Pete is always smiling, and he insists that a positive attitude is essential for leading a quality life. It's hard to argue with him on that point, but still his chronically upbeat orientation to the world seems a little forced. Sometimes you wonder if he's running from some greater pain, but he looks at you like you're crazy if you ask him about it. Most of the time his positive approach to life's problems is adaptive, but when things get very difficult he has a hard time letting himself feel grief, sadness, hopelessness, or any other normal human emotions. Pete often has extremely high standards for those around him and is equally intolerant of their own vulnerability, insisting that they should adopt a more positive attitude like his.

## EDDIE THE ESCAPE ARTIST

Eddie looks neither unhappy nor overly positive about life. He is an even-tempered guy who rarely gets too rattled about anything. Like Positive Pete, Eddie strives to avoid experiencing any painful emotions, but his MO is different. Rather than intentionally radiating a positive air whenever people are around, he does his best to keep things light by removing himself from any potentially unpleasant situations. Sometimes he retreats to his office or the workshop in the basement when there is any hint of conflict in the family. Other times he deftly changes the topic when conversations get a little too personal.

## BUSY BOB

Bob is so busy that he never has time to feel much of anything. The name of the game is staying active and on the move. While some people use drugs and alcohol to numb emotional pain, Bob uses constant activity. His inner pain may be particularly difficult to identify because his behavior seems so normal. In American culture he may even be applauded for his productivity and his commitment to work.

## NORMAL NATE

Nate does not deny that he is unhappy. Nor does he try to stay busy, adopt a positive attitude, or avoid family and friends. Instead, Nate is the kind of guy who says: "Of course I'm depressed. Who wouldn't be? My boss is a jerk, but I have to make a living. My family is under constant financial pressure, and I've had pain in my back 24-7 for the last five years. Plus I'm a guy. Guys don't talk about being depressed. That's just the way it is."

Nate hides in plain sight by normalizing his unhappiness, the situations that contribute to it, and his responses to both. So attempts to break through Nate's isolation are likely to come across as unjustified. After all, from Nate's perspective this is just the way things work, particularly when you're a guy.

## ATTITUDE AL

Al doesn't suffer fools gladly. All of his inner pain and suffering is channeled into the outward appearance of an angry man with an attitude. He argues frequently with friends, relatives, and even strangers if he thinks they're wrong about something important.

From Al's perspective, the problem is not that he is unhappy. The problem is that the world is screwed up; people don't do what they should, and no one can be trusted to follow through. As a result, Al has a long list of injustices he has experienced that he regularly turns over in his mind or with others if they're willing to listen.

The odds are good that you are familiar with one or more of these characters. If you are a man, you may even recognize parts of yourself. In the real world many men's approach to emotional pain is a combination of these various characters rather than a pure expression of one. Still, the questions remain: Why are so many men so heavily invested in hiding their pain? And why as a society are we so prepared not to see or hear it? In addition to what men learn about the hazards of expressing their inner pain, there is an important set of messages boys and men receive about what it means to "have a problem."

## SHAME AND THE MEANING OF "HAVING A PROBLEM"

Keeping control over your emotions is one of the most pervasive and powerful masculine norms to which boys and men are exposed. For many men the message is not only that you should keep your emotions under control, but that failure to do so is something to be ashamed of. As a result, many men believe that experiencing any sort of difficult emotions that cannot be quickly controlled is a sign of personal failure or weakness. Jerry, whom I mentioned earlier in this chapter, believed that in order to truly suffer from depression a person had to reach the point of giving up entirely. As he said to me, "The way I was raised, I was taught to soldier on. No matter how bad things get, you put one foot in front of the other and keep moving." From Jerry's perspective, being down, depressed, anxious, worried, or otherwise unhappy for more than a brief period of time was a sign of *failure* to soldier on. Therefore, Jerry had two major emotional problems to deal with: unrelenting unhappiness and the shame and self-blame always looming in the background due to his self-perceived failures to control his own emotions.

Adopting such a perspective on your own emotional pain often leads people into a sort of double-bind; not only do they experience repeated painful emotions, but they feel ashamed of their own emotional response.[16] Shame is different from guilt. We feel guilty when we judge our own *behavior* as having broken a moral code. We feel shame when we judge our *selves* to be unworthy of love, compassion, and social acceptance. People's natural response to shame is to want to hide themselves as much as possible so that the unwanted or rejected parts of the self cannot be seen and risk further rejection. Many men are able to report extremely shameful experiences of not living up to masculine norms of emotional control during their childhood. Crying and being called a "sissy," "wuss," or worse, is a classic example. Boys who express vulnerable emotions are often referred to as "momma's boys," "fags," and so on. The logic seems to be as follows:

> Expressing vulnerable emotions reflects a failure to control them.
> Failing to control them is shameful.
> It is shameful because it is not masculine.
> If it's not masculine to express vulnerable emotions, it must be feminine (ergo, misogynistic slurs).

If you scratch just slightly below the surface, none of these premises stand much scrutiny. For example, expressing vulnerable emotions does not necessarily mean that a person failed to control them; an individual may simply be comfortable expressing emotions and not restricted by the impulse to control them. Similarly, there is no reason that expressing vulnerable emotions necessarily needs to be considered "feminine" (and thus shameful for men). There are cultures and situations in which men's expressions of grief and sadness are considered entirely appropriate (such as tears at an Irish or Italian funeral).[17] Nonetheless, many men continue to feel extremely ashamed of the expression of vulnerable emotions except under rare circumstances.

Those things that we are ashamed of we also come to fear and avoid because they have been associated with very painful experiences in the past. When a person's own vulnerable emotions are the things they fear, the process of avoidance can become very rigid and ingrained. For example, one student at Clark University found in his thesis that men who scored higher on a measure of adherence to traditional masculine norms showed higher levels of fear while watching a film of a male character sobbing uncontrollably. What is particularly interesting is that these men did not report higher levels of fear. Rather, they demonstrated it physiologically with increased heart rate and higher levels of skin conductance. In other words, their bodies were revealing the fear they felt in the presence of a man sobbing while their minds were unable to detect that fear (or at least, if they did detect it, they were unable or unwilling to report it).

Along with polarizing lenses, shame can affect not only how men think about the meaning of having an emotional problem but also their thoughts about whether or not to share it with others. Research has demonstrated that men are far less likely than women, on average, to seek help from mental health care professionals. Men also report disclosing less to friends and family members. Men's reasons for preferring to keep problems to themselves are varied.[18] In our own research men often identify lack of time, financial constraints, and distrust of mental health care professionals as major obstacles to seeking help. But when we dig deeper several other more provocative themes begin to emerge. These include:

- Asking for help is admitting that I can't handle things on my own.
- Asking for help is giving up control to someone else.
- I'm not crazy, so I don't need help.
- I would be embarrassed for people to know that I was seeing a therapist.
- I don't want other people knowing my business because it could be used against me.
- What could a therapist/counselor do to help me when I'm stuck in a bad situation?
- Nobody knows more about my own problems than me, so how can anyone else help?
- Why should I go into all that deep stuff and risk falling apart when I'm doing fine now?

These sorts of concerns about seeking help reveal just how powerful is the pressure that many men feel to keep pain to themselves and to handle problems on their own.

## FLEXIBILITY: THE PATH TO CHANGE

A few years ago I gave a talk to local community members on what they can do to help teenage boys who are struggling with emotional problems. After I had reviewed several of the ideas covered in this chapter, a man in the audience raised his hand and said: "With all due respect, you keep saying we should help these boys to talk. But isn't it a good thing to be able to keep your feelings to yourself and handle problems on your own? I mean, aren't you sort of saying that men should become more like women and dump their feelings on everyone? What good is emotional diarrhea when it never helps you solve the problem anyway?"

This sort of reaction is not uncommon, and it reflects two major misunderstandings about the nature of men's silent pain. First, talking about what is happening in your life is not a "women's thing," and keeping quiet is not a "guy thing." As I said earlier, there is nothing inherently masculine about keeping quiet and nothing inherently feminine about sharing what is going on inside of you. Rather, it is the gender paradox that creates the *myth* that all men are naturally stoic, and all women are naturally emotionally dramatic. This myth, rather than inherent differences between men and women, is what makes many men afraid to share their inner lives. To become more open about what is really going on in your life is not about becoming more feminine; it is about becoming more human.

Second, I am not saying that it is *always* a good idea to share what is going on inside of you. There are plenty of situations in which it makes more sense to keep personal problems private; for example, when revealing them could later be used against you, or when revealing them could be too painful for you to bear at the time. On the other hand, it makes sense to share your personal problems with others when:

Doing so might allow you to receive needed support

Putting problems into words can help you see them more clearly

Bouncing things off someone else might help you see some new perspectives

The bottom line is that flexibility is a major key to human well-being. We do best when we are able to adapt how we approach problems in life to the situations in which we find ourselves, and to choose those approaches that have the greatest potential payoff. On the other hand, we are more likely to run into trouble when we are so wedded to one approach that we stick to it doggedly regardless of how helpful it is. Many men keep their inner lives silent and hidden not because it is really helpful to do so. They do it because that's what they were taught to do, that's what they've always done, that's what they see other men doing, and that's what seems normal. Similarly, many women accept men's silence and invisibility because that's what they've been taught to do and that's what they see around them every day. Just as men need to become more flexible in how they approach problems by learning to open up when it is helpful to do so, many women need to become more flexible in their openness to seeing and hearing what is really going on with the men in their lives. In the remainder of this chapter I suggest several different ways to make this happen.

## STOP, LOOK, AND LISTEN

You can often set yourself on a positive path to change by simply slowing down and paying attention to what's going on around you. I have shown throughout this chapter that in the case of men's silent and invisible emotional pain there is plenty to see and hear, provided that you know what to look and listen for. You can begin by taking inventory and asking yourself the following questions:

*Who are the important men in my life?* If you are a man, the list undoubtedly includes yourself. For both men and women, there are probably several other friends, family members, and significant others who are male. Over the next week, take a mental inventory of the men who are most important to you. Then ask yourself:

*How are the men in my life doing emotionally?* As we've seen, potential indicators of hidden pain in men's lives include substance abuse, anger, unexplained physical pains, and social isolation. When you take inventory consider whether any of the men in your life are expressing hidden pain in these ways. Or perhaps their distress is less hidden. Are they indicating in direct ways that they are struggling on the inside? In what ways might personal, private, and public silence be affecting these men?

*How can I better see and hear these men?* Whether you are concerned about yourself or other men in your life, there are probably steps you can take to better understand what's going on. Many of the communication strategies I described in the previous chapter can be helpful. It is also helpful to understand and empathize with the shame and fear that often accompany emotional distress in men. Remember that many men who are silently unhappy are struggling with the double problem I described earlier: not only are they unhappy, but their own unhappiness is an additional source of shame and self-blame.

*What are my own barriers to seeing men's emotional pain?* Most of us are raised in a society that considers men's emotional vulnerability shameful. As a result, we all develop barriers to seeing it. Regularly ask yourself how comfortable you are seeing and hearing about men's emotions. Simply posing the question to yourself will heighten your awareness and eventually help you to overcome the barriers. If you find yourself stuck and unable to get past your own discomfort, perhaps you are seeing men and their emotions through a polarizing lens. Or perhaps your own experiences growing up have produced certain beliefs about men and emotions that are so rigid that they are inhibiting your flexibility.

It seems like a cliché to say that change takes place one step at a time, and it may well be. But the fact is that it's true. The way we approach situations in our lives—day to day, hour to hour, and minute to minute—shapes the overall quality of our lives. Breaking through the silence and invisibility surrounding men's emotions is something you can practice every day in one way or another. Removing the polarizing lenses, stopping, looking, and listening—all of these things can help you take steps toward change in your daily life.

It is also important to remember that change is a gradual process; if it were easy to change, we would all be different because we would simply get rid of those parts of ourselves that we dislike for one reason or another. Recognizing that change is not easy does not mean you should throw up your hands and accept things as they are. Instead, it should lead you to adopt a patient and empathic stance toward those who are attempting to change, including yourself. Psychologists have identified some general strategies that help keep you on track in this regard. They include:

- Set small attainable goals rather than large ones, at least initially. This enhances the chances of success.
- Stay patient.
- Don't expect perfection; tolerate setbacks and keep moving forward.
- Learn to see change, no matter how small it is.
- Reinforce change when you see it by commenting on it positively.

## COMMUNICATING WITH YOURSELF:
## THE POWER OF WRITING

Even when, for a variety of reasons, a man may be unable or unwilling to talk with others directly about his private emotional life, he can still break through the silence and put himself on a healthier path. Writing about his own emotional experience is a very powerful way to do this.

For the past three decades the psychology professor James Pennebaker has been studying the effects of disclosing emotions in writing that are related to stressful or painful experiences that people go through. He and his colleagues have amassed a tremendous amount of scientific data showing that disclosing emotions by writing about them is associated with a wide range of health benefits.[19] In one early study Pennebaker and his colleagues encouraged two groups of people to write about either traumatic experiences or superficial experiences for four consecutive days. The results showed that those who wrote about traumatic experiences had better immune system functioning at a cellular level and fewer visits to a health center.

Since that early study there have been literally hundreds of follow-up studies demonstrating the positive effects of written emotional disclosure on outcomes ranging from enhanced memory capacity, to better mood regulation, to reduction of symptoms in patients with asthma.

Exactly why written emotional disclosure is beneficial is not clear. However, psychologists have speculated that writing about painful experiences helps individuals to make sense of them. Perhaps writing also allows us to confront feelings that cause us anxiety in much the same way that confronting high places can help someone with a fear of heights; the gradual exposure eventually helps a person feel less anxious and better able to confront what-ever things (heights, emotions) he or she previously avoided. On the other hand, continuing to put forth energy to avoid painful or uncomfortable feelings can eventually take a serious toll on our well-being.

Psychologists have also explored the possibility that our active attempts to avoid or suppress emotions can have harmful effects on our physical and mental health. (*Emotional suppression* is defined as conscious attempts to inhibit the expression of what a person is feeling.) The researcher James Gross and his colleagues, for example, have conducted several studies in which they instruct people to suppress what they are feeling after exposing them to something that should create strong feelings, such as a sad or dis-gusting movie. Their results show particular patterns of physiologi-cal activity when people try to suppress emotions. Moreover, studies have found that actively suppressing thoughts about painful emo-tions has negative effects on immunological functioning.[20]

Finally, researchers have discovered what they call an *ironic effect* of emotional suppression. For some people, particularly those who are already experiencing higher levels of distressing emotions (including anger), attempts to suppress those emotions actually increase them.[21] On the other hand, thinking too much about what you are feeling can also have negative effects. The psycholo-gist Susan Nolen-Hoeksema has conducted numerous studies that demonstrate that the tendency to think deeply and repeatedly about negative feelings puts people at risk for developing signifi-cant symptoms of depression. In other words, when people expe-rience painful emotions, focusing intensely on them for long periods of time can actually make them worse. Again, the bottom line is that flexibility and balance are the keys; thinking too much about what you are feeling, or actively trying to avoid what you are feeling, will produce negative effects on your emotional and physical health.

## SUMMARY

When it comes to emotional well-being, men and women are far more similar than they are different. In fact, the same holds true for the overwhelming majority of physical, social, and psychological characteristics that have been scientifically studied. We shouldn't be surprised, then, that men and women share 99.4 percent of their genetic makeup; the Y chromosome, which determines whether a fetus will develop into a male or a female, is by far the smallest of all the chromosomes. Yet our everyday commonsense experience seems to tell us that men and women are far more *different* than they are similar. This gender paradox creates the expectation that men *should* be different in the way they experience, express, and respond to their own emotions. Consequently, most men feel a tremendous amount of external and internal pressure to see and portray themselves as different from women. When problems in life arise that are perceived as "feminine," men can have a powerful sense of shame that leads them to hide their vulnerability to an even greater degree.

Men's tendency to see emotional experiences through polarizing lenses also restricts their flexibility in coping with difficult life situations by artificially sorting feelings and experiences into false oppositions (mental/physical, strong/weak, independent/dependent). Men's emotional vulnerabilities can be very difficult to see and hear because men are encouraged to keep them silent and invisible. As a result, individual men can often avoid dealing with emotional problems in their lives by adopting one of many socially accepted roles that normalize men's silent unhappiness (Grumpy Uncle Charlie, Solemn Sam, etc.).

To break through the silence surrounding men's well-being, all of us must take off the polarizing lenses that distort our perceptions of what's really going on with men. Once we do this, we are in a much better position to see men's real lives.

## · 6 ·

# Relationship Well-Being

There are probably more popular books, magazine articles, and Web sites dedicated to relationships than to any other aspect of men's well-being. Most of these outlets are designed for the partners of men—specifically, those partners who are unhappy with the quality of their intimate relationship. Help is provided by reassuring readers that the problems they are experiencing are not their own fault since, well, men are "wired differently" when it comes to relationships. For example: readers are often told:

- Men are not interested in emotional closeness.
- Men are obsessed with sex.
- Men's brains work differently from women's when it comes to relationships.

Readers are typically encouraged to give up the struggle and realize that their attempts to change men's behavior are doomed. Instead, they should accept how fundamentally different men are when it comes to relationships—and find ways to accommodate these differences.

You may have already detected the polarizing lenses that frame these ideas. And as you've probably guessed by this point, I take a different perspective on men in intimate relationships. Although polarizing lenses encourage us all to see men as fundamentally different from women, research shows that most men *want* the same things in intimate relationships as do all human beings: closeness, companionship, fun, family, emotional support, and so on.[1] Yet while men's true desires in relationships may be quite similar to women's, shame and fear make it very difficult for many men to allow their needs to be seen and heard by their partners. Sometimes the shame and fear are so strong that men themselves are unaware of their own needs and desires in relationships.

This chapter is about how men's silence and invisibility affect the quality of intimate relationships. Throughout the chapter I use the generic term *partner* (or *partners*) when I want to talk about intimate relationships in general. Statistically speaking, the majority of men's partners are women. However, men involved with other men in intimate relationships often face many of the same issues, and, in fact, at times these issues can be that much more powerful when two men are involved.

## PATTERNS OF SILENCE AND INVISIBILITY
## BETWEEN PARTNERS

Silence and invisibility can take several different forms in intimate relationships. Some people feel completely shut out from their partner's inner lives, and this can take a heavy toll on closeness in the relationship. Consider how familiar the following conversation is, if not in your own relationship then in the relationships you have observed.

PARTNER: How was your day?

MAN: Fine.

PARTNER: How did it go at work?

MAN: Nothing new really.

PARTNER: But weren't you going to talk to your boss about the stuff that happened last week? Did you talk to him? What did he say?

MAN: I talked to him. He didn't say much.

PARTNER: Well, how are you feeling about all of this?

MAN: What do you mean?

PARTNER: I want to know what's going on with you. How are you feeling about the problems at work and other stuff?

MAN: I don't know what you want from me.

Of course, what his partner wants from him, and what many people want from their male partners, is emotional intimacy. Emotional intimacy is created when *vulnerability exists between people in the context of a safe relationship.*[2] In other words, to feel close to someone often requires that you put yourself in a vulnerable position. Women often learn that one effective way to do this is to talk about their feelings or problems in life with another person. Men typically learn exactly the opposite: making yourself vulnerable by talking about problems or feelings does not always lead to intimacy; it can easily produce shame, rejection, or humiliation. The end result is that many people involved in intimate relationships with men crave intimacy through verbal sharing; the very thing that many men are deeply afraid of.

There is also the opposite end of the spectrum. A man will share *all* of his inner life with his partner, and not with anyone else. His partner can then become overburdened by the responsibility of being *the one person* who sees and hears a man's true inner life. I once worked with a forty-four-year-old woman, Lisa, who had married her high school sweetheart, Mark. Lisa had come to see me because she was worried about Mark. She thought he might be extremely depressed, and Mark refused to seek any sort of counseling or medication. It was getting to the point where Lisa was worried about their marriage. Mark was, in many ways, a "guy's guy." He worked in construction during the week and enjoyed pickup softball games and cookouts on the weekends. Mark had kept the same group of friends since high school, and neither he nor Lisa had ever moved away from their hometown.

I asked Lisa what sort of support Mark had other than her. "He has tons of friends that he sees every weekend," Lisa said.

I asked her if Mark talked with them about feeling depressed. Lisa didn't know, but she agreed to ask him as part of her homework before our next session. When Lisa came back the following week, she reported that Mark had said: "Of course I don't talk to them about feeling depressed. Why would I? Those guys like to have fun. And they know me as the sort of person who keeps things light. You know me, I'm always joking around. I don't think they'd be too interested. Plus, I've got you to talk to. You know that you have always been my best friend, and I can tell you anything. I don't know what I'd do without you." Lisa went on to say: "You know, it makes me feel really good that he trusts me that much. I mean I am glad that he feels comfortable talking to me, and he always has. But it's like, jeez, you know, am I everything he has? He needs more than that."

I asked Lisa what she needed from Mark given that he was struggling with some major issues in his life. She looked away and cast her eyes down; a classic indicator of guilt or shame. Then she told me: "It seems incredibly selfish to say this, especially when he is the one who is dealing with so much. But to be honest with you, I need him to not rely on me so much to talk about how bad he feels. I feel like I am the holder of this incredibly big secret that no one else knows about. And I'm not supposed to tell anyone because he needs to save face around his friends. It makes me wonder what would happen to him if we did split up."

Lisa's fears were not unfounded. Research has shown that women are more likely than men to initiate divorce, and men tend to fare worse emotionally following divorce.[3-6] It is not entirely clear why. However, one contributing factor may be that men have much less support available to them after divorce. It makes sense. If a man tends to keep all of his "emotional eggs" in one basket, when that basket is no longer available he can quickly become isolated. The bottom line is that under the right circumstances, men's private silence is capable of creating a tremendous burden for their partners. Ironically, many men think they are doing their partners a favor by keeping it to themselves.

Unlike Lisa, some partners are not interested in hearing *anything* about men's private struggles. If a partner believes that men should be strong, silent, and emotionally stoic, she or he is unlikely to be prepared for a man who wants to talk about his inner vulnerabilities. Particularly for partners with many other stressors (such as family or work), it can be a relief to be with a man who handles all of his problems on his own. This is a delicate balance to maintain because there is often a fine line between avoiding burdening someone you love, on the one hand, and creating too much emotional distance, on the other.

## WHAT IS IT LIKE TO BE SILENT AND INVISIBLE IN AN INTIMATE RELATIONSHIP?

It is fairly common for people in a relationship with a silent or invisible man to see his behavior as intentional. It can seem like he's withholding himself on purpose, trying to keep the upper hand, choosing not be close, and so on. The man in turn often feels criticized and defensive. From his perspective, "I'm simply doing what I do," and there is no conscious intention to reject or otherwise hurt his partner. This sort of standstill can be very frustrating and painful for both partners in a relationship.

People who study the dynamics of how couples interact will tell you that the first step toward overcoming an impasse like this is stopping the blame game. In other words, rather than focusing on who is at fault, or who has bad intentions, focus your attention instead on what it feels like to be stuck in the situation.[7] Partners are often very clear on what their own anger feels like. But they are often not clear on their own vulnerability. Even less clear is what it *actually feels like* to be silent and invisible in a relationship.

### EXERCISE: PRACTICE HIDING WHAT YOU FEEL

To really get a sense of what it is like to be silent and invisible, you need to actually try it. If you are someone who generally feels comfortable sharing what is going on inside of you, this can seem extremely awkward—and that's the point. It *is* awkward and unnatural. In fact it is remarkable that for so many men it has become commonplace. Nonetheless, as I have said before, empathy is critical for change; you must be able to know what it is like to keep your emotional life hidden from view if you want to help yourself, or those you care about, to change.

My colleagues Holly Sweet and Lea Perlman developed a very creative and powerful exercise to help people understand what many men go through when they render themselves silent and invisible. They use this exercise—called the *stiff upper lip*—in workshops for men and women, but you can also try it on your own with a friend or relative. The first step is to think of a time in your life when you felt sad. Try to remember an event that can still create that feeling of sadness. Take a couple of minutes to close your eyes and visualize the event. Focus on what it felt like to be there.

Now open your eyes and tell the other person about the event and what it felt like to experience it. However, you must follow this rule: *you are not allowed to let any of the sadness show.* Make jokes about it whenever possible. If the other person responds with any kind of concern, blow it off as "no big deal."

Can you imagine behaving this way on a regular basis when you talk about important events in your life? One of the things you may have noticed is how much effort it takes to actively keep your feelings hidden. For some men the process has reached the point of becoming a habit, yet still it takes effort. And as I discussed in the previous chapter, the consequences—at a physiological as well as a psychological level—can take a serious toll over time.

## EXERCISE: HOW DOES IT FEEL BEING ON THE RECEIVING END OF SILENCE?

Now is a good time to do some self-assessment about how men's silence and invisibility might play a role in your own relationship. If you are not currently in an intimate relationship, you can still learn some things about yourself and your relationship patterns by doing the exercise as if you were. It might help to think about the last time you were in a close relationship. The goal is to get a sense of what happens when your partner tends to keep privately, personally, or publicly silent.

Which of the following words best describes how you feel when your partner keeps his problems to himself?

| | |
|---|---|
| worried | happy |
| angry | sad |
| conflicted | anxious |
| relieved | upset |
| nothing | safe |

Perhaps your response depends on the situation, the type of problem he is experiencing, or how the relationship is going at the time. If that's the case, try completing the following sentences with the first thing that comes to mind.

I do not mind my partner keeping problems to himself if:

On the other hand, it bothers me if he keeps problems to himself when:

What do you notice about your responses? Some people are surprised to learn the range or intensity of their feelings about their partner's silence and invisibility. It is one thing to know that loving an excessively quiet man can be frustrating. It is another to appreciate that at times it might make you feel scared, anxious, worried, or angry.

If you would like to learn more about where these feelings are coming from, it helps to consider the thoughts that can give rise to them. Often, if we are feeling a particular way, it's because we are imagining something, predicting something, or believing that something is going to happen. Here is a list of thoughts that might be driving some of your feelings about your partner's silence and invisibility.

| If I feel: | It might be because: |
| --- | --- |
| Worried | I am predicting something bad is going to happen if he doesn't open up more. |
| Angry | I think he *should* be acting differently and sharing more with me. |
| Conflicted | I am not sure how I feel about his keeping quiet. There are advantages and disadvantages to it. |
| Relieved | I am somewhat afraid of what I would hear or see if he shared more of his inner life with me. |
| Sad | I think his silence means that he does not love me, or that we are not as close as we should be. |
| Safe | I think if he were to open up to me more, bad things might happen (e.g., I might feel overwhelmed). |

If you think he would be open to hearing about it, you might consider sharing some of your responses with your partner. In my experience, many men think that they are doing their partners a favor by keeping their inner lives hidden. They do not realize that this kind of excessive privacy can actually create fear, anger, sadness, or other painful feelings for their partners. On the other hand, if this is a familiar topic of discussion in your relationship, you might elicit defensiveness from your partner if you share your responses with him.

One exception is if you typically only express anger to your partner, and this exercise has helped you to realize that his silence also leads you to experience sadness, fear, or other vulnerable feelings. Nine times out of ten, sharing vulnerable feelings with a partner, as opposed to anger, is a better way to go in relationships. It is far less threatening to hear about, and it has the potential to create intimacy where previously there was only conflict.

If you are a man who tends to keep your inner life silent and invisible, you may find it difficult to understand how it can be painful and frustrating for your partner. As already noted, you may think that you are doing your partner a favor by sparing him or her the burden of your own problems. Perhaps you were raised in a family where keeping quiet about one's emotional life was the norm. If so, it may not make much sense to you that someone would want to know about all the conflict that goes on inside you. What is crucial for the quality of your relationship is not that you and your partner approach things the same way, but rather that you and your partner have empathy and respect for each other's approach.

Toward that end, it may be helpful for you to spend some time thinking about what it would be like to be in your partner's shoes: Imagine having a good friend with whom you share some very important interests (perhaps sports, hobbies, business issues, or politics). Talking about things with your friend gives you a strong sense of companionship, so much so that you look forward to getting together on a regular basis. Now imagine that for whatever reason this person no longer wants to talk about these topics with you; they are simply off-limits. How might you feel in response? Frustrated? Hurt? Uncertain about where you stand or how important you are to this person? These are the very same reactions many partners have when the men they are involved with keep their inner lives to themselves.

## THE ORIGINS OF SILENCE IN RELATIONSHIPS

In part 1, I talked about working with the psychologist Marsha Linehan while I was in graduate school. I also had the good fortune to work with one of the world's experts on couples and couples therapy, the late Neil Jacobson. Neil dedicated his career to the scientific study of couples' relationships. He also had a keen intuitive sense about the dynamics of intimate relationships. As just one example, Neil met with the graduate students as a group on a weekly basis to review their couples therapy sessions on videotape. It was not unusual for him to stop the tape, point out something subtle about what the couple was doing, and predict how they would behave in the next five minutes. Most of the time he was right.

During the last phase of his career, Neil began to study the nature of intimacy and emotional vulnerability between people in close relationships. He had begun to realize, and the scientific data were also showing him, that closeness in relationships depends on a certain degree of emotional intimacy, which, in turn, depends on people's ability to share vulnerable emotions with each other. Neil observed, for example, that when many couples fight there are strong vulnerable feelings (e.g., fear, sadness, anxiety) underlying the anger. Often, simply identifying these more vulnerable feelings and sharing them with a partner promotes much greater closeness and less conflict than arguing about the more surface issues.

Like Marsha Linehan, Neil had not incorporated research on the specific psychology of men into his work. Tragically, he died at a relatively young age, just around the time I was becoming interested in this area. I regret that we were never able to talk about the issues this book addresses and how they relate to understanding and promoting intimacy in couples.

Neil often noted that the men in relationships struggle more than women to experience and express more vulnerable emotions. The students all agreed that this pattern exists, but never stopped to ask *why* it exists. Here was another example of rendering men's vulnerability silent and invisible. Now, close to twenty years later, it seems much clearer to me. And seeing where it comes from, clearly and compassionately, is the first step toward breaking the silence.

Many psychologists believe that men's silence in intimate relationships traces back to their early childhood. In part 1, I described our society's expectations that men be tough, stoic, independent, and so on. This societal pressure affects how parents interact with their young sons: not only do parents feel compelled to encourage their sons to "act like boys" in order for the young children to "become men" but also, and unfortunately, parents may unknowingly encourage young boys' rejection of their own needs for emotional closeness, intimacy, and mutual dependence in relationships.

In his book *Real Boys*, William Pollack discusses research demonstrating that young male infants and toddlers are actually more emotional than their female counterparts. However, by the time they reach middle childhood many boys' more vulnerable emotions seem to have gone underground. Pollack and other researchers and theorists in the psychology of men believe that this tendency is driven by excessive societal pressure for boys to prematurely separate from their primary emotional connection, which is usually their mother.[8] The pressure to "not be a mama's boy" leads many young boys to feel ashamed of their desires for emotional closeness, intimacy, safety, and dependence. Pollack and others suggest that for many men the result of these childhood experiences is an adult fear of their own emotional vulnerability. The fear is not necessarily a conscious one. For some men it may be more of an ingrained habit; an automatic "don't-go-there" response when potential emotional closeness and vulnerability come together.

This recent work in the psychology of men goes a long way toward explaining why so many men keep their inner lives silent and invisible in close relationships. And here we come to a point I cannot emphasize enough: *Although many adult men fear emotional closeness and intimacy, that doesn't mean they don't desire it.* When men are asked confidentially what they want out of intimate relationships, they report largely the same desires as women. On the other hand, the stereotype is that all men want is sex and that it's women who are the ones lobbying for more discussion, more sharing, and so on. Perhaps when couples get to the point of repeated conflict they end up polarized around these issues, and I will have more to say about that when I consider the demand-withdraw pattern later in this chapter. For now, it is worth considering the fact that most men do desire emotional closeness in relationships.

You may be wondering if it is possible for two people in a relationship to have very different notions about what exactly brings them closer together and what it feels like to be close. The answer is yes; it certainly is possible and probably fairly common. What is unfortunate is that so many partners in relationships never get to the point of actually talking about what makes each of them feel close. For men, there are many obstacles to having this sort of conversation.

First, many men do not feel competent when it comes to discussing emotions in a close relationship. They may have been raised with the notion that "women do that kind of thing." They may also have had repeated experiences in their adult relationships in which they felt inferior in comparison to a partner who was much better at these sorts of interactions. Feeling incompetent at *anything* goes against one of the most basic rules of traditional masculinity: always know what you're doing, know how to do it well, and perform when expected to.

Second, many men fear that revealing their truer, more vulnerable selves will result in shame and humiliation from their partners. If you are in an intimate relationship with a man whom you love, trust, and strive to support, you may find it baffling that he could actually think that you would humiliate or shame him for sharing his feelings. Bear in mind that his fear of shame and humiliation may not be rooted in your current relationship as much as it is driven by his earlier developmental experiences with sharing vulnerable emotions; as I discussed earlier, many men's needs for closeness, dependence, and emotional intimacy were shamed out of them as young boys when they were taught to toughen up, quit crying for Mommy, and so on. Also note that sometimes the fear of being shamed and humiliated does come to fruition even when that is by no means the intended result. A friend of mine had an interaction with his wife that illustrates this process precisely.

My friend and I were discussing the psychological research on predictors of happiness in couples' relationships. I speculated that if more men were able to have their inner lives seen and heard by their partners, perhaps we would see lower rates of divorce and higher rates of marital satisfaction and intimacy. Since my colleague and I tend to think about people in very similar ways, I assumed that he would readily agree. Instead he said, "Are you kidding? Women don't want to hear about that stuff."

"What do you mean?" I asked. "They'd sure rather hear about a guy hurting than about how pissed off he is all the time."

My colleague looked at me as if I were a little boy, and truly clueless about what women really want. Then he said:

Let me tell you what happened the other day. I'd been having one of those days at work where nothing was turning out the way it was supposed to. Ordinarily, I'd be pissed off, I'd drink more coffee than usual, maybe be cranky with my wife when I spoke to her on the phone. But I guess all this stuff we've been talking about got to me, and I decided to see what it would be like to follow your advice. So I sat quietly for a couple of minutes and tried to let go of the anger. You know, get in touch with the more vulnerable stuff. I realized that I was afraid these projects weren't going to work out; I was going to be held responsible, there were going to be bad financial consequences, and so on. Pretty soon I realized that I was actually pretty anxious about how things were going. So when I called my wife, instead of saying what I usually would ("I'm pissed off, having a shitty day, what's up with you?"), I decided to tell her about the other feelings. And that's what I did. Laid the whole thing out for her, the anxiety, all my fears, et cetera. You know what she said? "Why are you laying all this on me?" Hell if that didn't shut me up fast. Why was I laying it on her?! I wasn't laying anything on. I was trying to be honest. Like I said, I just don't think women want to hear about this stuff.

I had to wipe a smile from my face when my friend finished speaking, not because I was laughing at him but because his story was so familiar. Members of a couple often miss each other entirely when they're trying to do things in a new way; one person decides to take a risk in the relationship, the other is caught off guard, doesn't know how to respond, and both people end up hurt and confused.

There were also a number of illogical inferences in my friend's account of his interaction with his wife. He assumed, for example, that because his wife responded negatively to what he had shared, she would always react that way. My colleague also generalized from his wife to all women ("I just don't think women want to hear about this stuff"). It was like dipping his toe in the water at the edge of the pool, finding it too cold, and deciding never to swim again. On the other hand, it was clear to me that he found the water more than a little cold; his wife's dismissal of his private turmoil hit him hard and made him very reluctant to share similar things with her in the future. Finally, knowing his wife fairly well, I was also quite certain that she had no intention of shaming or humiliating him. She was probably caught off guard and didn't know quite how to respond. This was unfamiliar territory for both my friend and his wife.

The psychologist Stephen Bergman coined the term *relational dread* to describe the third factor underlying men's fear of the various ways things can go wrong when you make yourself vulnerable in an intimate relationship.[9] Bergman suggests that many men have a sense of impending doom when the topic of "our relationship" arises in couples. He describes it as a "deep sense of dread, a visceral sense, literally in the gut, or heart. Invitation starts to seem like demand, urgency and curiosity like criticism. The more the woman [*sic*] comes forward, offering to explore things relationally, the more the man feels dread and wants to avoid things relationally." Bergman identifies several characteristics of relational dread, including a sense of:

The inevitability of disaster (nothing good can come of it)

Timelessness (it will never end)

Impending damage (harmful effects will come from it)

Incompetence and shame (I am no good at this, and I should be better)

I think Bergman is on to something, but I would take it one step farther: the dread is not only of focusing on the relationship per se but also of any situation in which vulnerable emotions might be shared with another person. Because intimacy requires a degree of vulnerability, it's probably not too far a stretch to say that many men can come to dread intimacy. As I said earlier, it is not that men lack the desire for closeness, but rather that the experience of emotional vulnerability, which often goes along with it, is a heavily charged experience for many men.

Finally, there is another pattern in intimate relationships that contributes to men's silence and invisibility. It is so common that scientists who study couples' interactions have given it a name: the demand-withdraw pattern. One partner in the relationship typically makes demands for more discussion of a problem, more intimacy, or otherwise more engagement between the two. This prompts the other partner to withdraw, which only leads the first partner to demand more. And so the cycle continues.

The psychology professor Andrew Christensen has been studying the demand-withdraw pattern for over twenty-five years.[10-11] His findings and those of other researchers are remarkably consistent. First, the demand-withdraw pattern is associated with more conflict and less intimacy in marriages. Second, there is a consistent gender difference. As you might guess, women are more likely to be in the demanding role, and men are more likely to be in the withdrawing role. This means that women who are involved with men who tend to keep their inner lives to themselves are, on average, going to be more likely to try to draw those very men out. And these attempts are likely to have exactly the opposite effect of the one desired; they tend to make men even more withdrawn. On the other hand, much depends on how different men are approached.

There are effective ways to help men open up, which I will discuss in the next section.

## SEEING AND HEARING MEN IN RELATIONSHIPS

I have emphasized the importance of intimacy in relationships at several points in this chapter. The challenge, of course, is that simply telling your partner "Let's have more intimacy in our relationship" doesn't necessarily do the trick, and it may well backfire. If your partner is a man, the word *intimacy* itself may have a charged history; recall that men are taught to avoid anything that might be considered feminine, and historically, with the exception of sex, many men associate the various connotations of *intimacy* with femininity.

How, then, can a person learn to promote greater closeness and intimacy with a man when these are often the very things he fears? The short answer is that simply recognizing, respecting, and empathizing with his fear and ambivalence can promote greater closeness. The more you understand about the way men's silence and invisibility work in close relationships, without necessarily being judgmental, the more you will naturally create the conditions for intimacy in your own relationship. In other words, *truly seeing and hearing men's struggles with emotional intimacy is a great way to promote closeness.* When you begin to do this on a regular basis you will find that the typical power struggles couples get into, such as the demand-withdraw pattern, become less common. Greater closeness and a better sense of mutual understanding can then emerge in other areas of your relationship. Here are seven things you can do to help make this happen.

## 1. REMEMBER THE GENDER PARADOX

One of the great paradoxes of gender is that men and women are far more similar than they are different, yet common sense tells us that they are different. Remember that most men desire closeness in intimate relationships, even though they may not be able to ask for it and may be uncomfortable when it gets to be too much. If you remember this, you will be more likely to:

- Stop blaming men for having difficulty with emotional intimacy.
- Realize that most men do not try to be silent and invisible in close relationships out of a desire to hurt their partners. Rather, this is the default position they have learned over time from a society that defines masculinity in ways that can make it hard for individual men to get close.
- Stop believing pop psychology books and other exaggerated claims that men and women are "wired completely differently." Such claims are far overstated. In the short run they may help you to become less frustrated with your partner, but in the long run they prevent you from seeing his true self.
- Figure out the things you can do in your own relationship to better see your partner's inner life, and to experience greater levels of closeness and intimacy as a result.

## 2. LEAVE SHAME AND CRITICISM OUT OF THE EQUATION

Shame and criticism shut down communication in close relationships. They cause one or both people to become self-protective, and in the case of invisible men, to hide their inner lives even further. To promote closeness and allow your partner to share more of himself with you, you need to avoid shame and criticism whenever possible. This includes the shame and criticism that you may heap on yourself. Some people, for example, begin to feel ashamed of their own need for closeness when their partner does not regularly reciprocate. ("Maybe it's *my* problem, and I should just get over it.") But just as you need to respect a man's difficulty in having his inner life be seen and heard, you need to respect your own desire to see and hear it.

You can help yourself and your partner to use shame and criticism less frequently by recognizing what triggers this response. Typically, we become shaming and critical when we feel threatened or hurt; it is a form of lashing out to protect ourselves. At such times, it helps to stop, take a deep breath, and ask yourself, "What is threatening to me right now? What is hurting me?" Rather than lashing out at your partner, or attacking yourself and your own needs, try simply recognizing what you are feeling, and perhaps sharing it with your partner. Again, vulnerability, rather than anger, is more likely to promote closeness and understanding in relationships.

## 3. REMEMBER THAT CLOSENESS COMES IN MANY DIFFERENT FORMS

The things that help you to feel close to your partner may not be the same things that work for him. Talking, doing activities together (such as going to the movies, hiking, sightseeing on vacation, having sex, spending time with family), sharing interests, and a host of other things can help people feel close in an intimate relationship. The key is to figure out what works for each partner, and to avoid judging whose approach is "right." For example, there is nothing inherently more intimate about talking with each other versus taking a walk. Some men feel closer to their partners when they are engaged in a common activity than when they are sitting face-to-face talking about their feelings or the struggles in their lives. Judging a man as shallow because he prefers action over discussion will only lead him to feel defensive and become more silent and invisible.

## 4. GIVE UP THE POWER STRUGGLE

The demand-withdraw pattern keeps its momentum going through power struggles; the more one person demands intimacy, the more the other withdraws. If you tend to make more and more requests for closeness when you feel distanced from your partner, you are probably making the problem worse. Before you can turn things around, you need to recognize this pattern and make a commitment to changing it. You might say to your partner: "I don't want to pressure you, and I don't want to push you away. I know that the more I tell you I want to be close, I want to share, I want to spend time together, the more pressured you feel and the more boundaries you need to put up. So I'm not going to pressure you anymore. At the same time, it's important to me that you know how I feel. I do want to be close to you. I want to feel connected, and I hope that we can talk about how to help this happen without you feeling pressured or criticized." Your partner may not respond immediately, but avoiding getting into the demand-withdraw pattern is a critical first step in allowing greater closeness to emerge.

If you are a man who tends to get into power struggles about intimacy and closeness, ask yourself why you are withdrawing from your partner. What is it about your partner's desire to see and hear about your inner life that is leading you to shut down? Is relational dread playing a role? Perhaps your own discomfort with letting your vulnerable emotions be seen and heard is getting in the way. If you are unsure whether it is a good idea to open up a bit more, consider the pros and cons of doing so. Examine the effects of keeping quiet on your relationship. For example, how does your partner respond when you keep it all "under the hood"?

## 5. KEEP MOM TO A MINIMUM

Many boys are pressured to separate from their caregivers (typically mothers) too early in their development. As a result, they not only fear closeness and intimacy but also long for the sort of intense dependency and connection that exist in a mother-child relationship. When they become men they may continue to be ambivalent about this sort of connection because the loss of it was so painful as a child.

For a subset of these men, the model of an intimate relationship with a woman is having all their needs anticipated and met in the way a mother might do for a child. When women find themselves in a relationship with men such as these, they may unknowingly fall into the "mothering" role. Although this sort of mother-child dynamic can temporarily promote intimacy in the relationship, it typically comes at a cost. Men often come to fear and resent the very thing they long for when this dynamic arises; they may feel infantilized out of shame over their own dependency. Women eventually recognize that the pattern exists and begin to resent their role in it. As with many of the things I've discussed in this book, flexibility is the key. A little bit of mother-child dynamic now and then is not detrimental to a relationship. The problems arise when it becomes the only way for intimacy to exist between two people.

## 6. GET OUTSIDE YOUR COMFORT ZONE

The devil you know often seems safer than the unknown, whatever that may be. Particularly in longer-term relationships, partners in a couple often settle into habitual ways of behaving toward each other. These habits can include ways of expressing closeness, ways of managing conflict, or more mundane patterns related to watching television, sleeping, and so on. Although many of our relationship habits develop because they serve useful purposes, we can also get stuck in ruts. Sometimes these ruts are self-protective. For example, I once worked with a couple who had suffered the blow of one of their children dying at a young age. Although they grieved heavily at the time of the loss, they hadn't spoken about the child in years. Their habit was to simply keep quiet on such a potentially painful topic. Their silence was self-protective because it kept them from feeling additional pain related to the loss. However, it was also destructive for their relationship since it prevented them from sharing their loss together and being sources of emotional support for each other. I encouraged them each to step outside their comfort zone and experiment with discussing the topic, simply to see what would happen. As it turned out, they found the conversation to be a huge relief. All of that energy they had used trying to avoid the topic could now be put to better purposes.

## 7. NOTICE SIGNS OF SILENT AND INVISIBLE PAIN

Some men express emotional struggles in ways that mask their own vulnerability. Anger, substance abuse, physical aches and pains, increased stress, and other general physical symptoms can all be signs of underlying unhappiness. If you are involved in a close relationship with such a man, it can be difficult to know what's really going on. You may suspect that he is struggling privately but find yourself unable to find a way to talk to him about it. He may even reject your attempts to provide emotional support by insisting that nothing is wrong, or attributing the problems entirely to external circumstances ( "Yes, I'm stressed, but as soon as this deal comes through everything will be fine").

Try not to be too put off if you find yourself on the receiving end of statements such as these. Although your partner may not be able to acknowledge his own struggles, and on the surface it may seem as if he does not want your support, the odds are very good that he does want it. The challenge for a partner of a man like this is to find ways to be supportive while still allowing him to be in control of how he approaches his situation. For example, it is not helpful to insist that he acknowledge that he is unhappy, worried, sad, or otherwise. Simply saying "I'm concerned about you; let me know if you want to talk" can go a long way toward letting a man know that you are there for him while still allowing him to save face and approach his own inner life in a way that feels relatively safe. You might even consider leaving him a brief note expressing your love, concern, and availability should he want to connect. Again, the goal is to be there for him while not overly "mothering" him or otherwise pushing him too hard to experience his own vulnerability.

## SUMMARY

There are many myths about the differences between men and women in close relationships. One of the most pervasive is the notion that men are not interested in emotional closeness and intimacy. The fact is that many men desire closeness with their partners but are simultaneously afraid of it and ashamed of their own desires for it. Some men may attempt to cope with their fear and shame by staying silent and invisible within a close relationship. Other men experience relational dread, a powerful sense that nothing good can come of making yourself vulnerable to another person.

Breaking this pattern requires us all to see, hear, and respect men's struggles with intimacy. You can begin by carefully assessing your own reactions when men you are close to do not engage with you in the way you want them to. Men can assess their own concerns about making themselves more vulnerable and judge the pros and cons of continuing to stay hidden. Once individuals own their own issues regarding men's silence and invisibility in relationships, change becomes possible. Clear, nonjudgmental, and empathic communication is key. Some helpful guidelines include paying attention to the gender paradox and polarizing lenses, leaving shame and criticism out of conversations, being open to multiple forms of closeness and intimacy, keeping "mothering" to a minimum, and periodically stepping outside your comfort zone.

# 7

# Silence and Invisibility in Men's Friendships

## "YOU'RE DOING WELL IF . . ."

Sometimes there is a fine line between a simple observation and a profound piece of advice. When I was thirteen years old my family had just moved for the fourth time in five years, including once across the country and twice into new school districts. Again I faced the familiar challenge of making new friends. I was also figuring out what to wear, what to say, how to walk, and all of the other social norms that are so powerful for emerging adolescents. This time was particularly challenging because we had moved to the very edge of a wealthy West Los Angeles school district. Our family was decidedly middle class, while many of my peers were sons and daughters of actors, musicians, and corporate executives. They also implicitly understood the rules of the laid-back surfer culture that dominated the time and place. They hung out at the beach, wore cool surfer clothing, and never looked too bothered about anything one way or the other. On the other hand, having been born in Oklahoma, I was just four years out of cowboy boots, bolo ties, and a decidedly uncool southern accent. My head was constantly full of worries. *Does that boy think I'm a dork? Will these people ever like me? Am I going to drown if I try to surf?* In short, making friends was an uphill battle.

These days it is fairly common for teenage boys and girls to develop platonic friendships. But in the mid-1970s, gender segregation among friends was more the norm. As a result, if I wanted to have friends at school, it was clearly going to be a matter of developing relationships with other boys. So I pressured my parents into buying me a subscription to *Surfer* magazine and read every page, trying desperately to find a common language with my peers. I tried growing my hair long, but unfortunately it only grew "big." And no matter how many hours I lay in the sun, my English, Polish, and Russian DNA was not going to allow me much of a tan. So I pretended that I didn't need anyone, that I didn't care about anything but surfing the most radical waves, and that I was perfectly content being an outsider. Of course, on the inside I was desperately lonely and wanted nothing more than to be as happy, carefree, and surrounded by friends as all the other boys seemed to be.

One evening at dinner my parents asked how my day was, and for some unknown reason I decided to tell the truth. Tears poured out as I confessed to eating lunch alone, sitting by myself on the bus, and living day to day with a deep-rooted sense that there must be something wrong with me. I expected my parents to try to cheer me up by telling me it takes time; things will work out, and so on. But neither of them said much, instead choosing to listen and be supportive. Eventually, when I was all cried out, my father turned toward me and leaned forward. I will never forget the palpable sorrow in his eyes. "Son," he said, "I wish this wasn't true. But the fact is, if you make two close friends in your life, you're doing well."

To this day, I don't know whether my father intended this to be an observation or a piece of advice. On the one hand, there seemed to be a golden nugget of truth in what he said. Many years later, in fact, I discovered that the father of one of my closest friends told him the same thing at about the same age. What are the odds of that? Perhaps this was some kind of accumulated historical wisdom passed from one generation of men to another. Don't expect much when it comes to friendship. Be glad for what you have because you could have nothing. On the other hand, my father's statement also seemed like a cop-out. Why should boys and men live in such isolation from each other? And what about the groups of five, ten, fifteen boys I saw together every day, laughing and teasing each other around the lunch tables? Were they not close friends? As an adult now, living in New England, I have met many men who have extended networks of friends that trace back to high school or earlier. They gather at weekly golf outings, annual camping trips, and in some cases their families have become friendly as well. Are these men not close friends? Was my father offering an accurate and sober assessment of men's friendships? Or was his message severely skewed by his own struggle between isolation and the desire for greater closeness with other men?

I have come to think that my father's statement was *both* an observation and a piece of advice. Like many of the traditional masculine norms I identified in part I, there was a strong component of "should" in his statement. If it is true that most men are lucky to make two close friends in their life, this suggests a lot about how we *should* feel, think, and act with regard to close friendships in general. Perhaps we should not get our hopes up so we're never disappointed. Or maybe we should never get too close to anyone since the odds of any relationship turning into a close friendship are so slim. Or perhaps the message is to cherish the few friends we do make and do everything we can to keep them. On the other hand, one thing we definitely should *not* do is expect to feel close to more than a handful of other men.

This chapter is about the ways silence and invisibility in men's lives create the very struggles my father unknowingly identified. For the majority of the chapter I focus on same-sex friendships between men because these are often the relationships where men face the greatest obstacles in creating and maintaining closeness. At the same time, men's friendships with women are extremely important; many heterosexual men, for example, consider their wife or partner their best friend. As I mentioned in the previous chapter, this can be a source of great closeness for couples, and it can also be a significant burden for women; in effect, many women become the primary emotional caretakers for the men in their lives.

## THE PROS AND CONS OF ISLAND LIVING

Men often face a dilemma when it comes to friendships with other men. On the one hand, they may desire closeness, companionship, and intimacy with other men. On the other hand, most men learn that they can only expect this to happen with a handful of men in their lives, if they are even that fortunate. Some men choose to resolve the dilemma by staying silent and invisible and never really getting close to anyone. They may have numerous "buddies" with whom they share activities, but things stay relatively superficial. No one has to risk getting close and being hurt or disappointed. Other men live their entire lives longing for greater closeness and never finding it. They may not even be aware of their desires, although they are regularly visited by a powerful sense of isolation, disconnection, and longing around other men. And then some men are fortunate enough to create and maintain close relationships with other men. For these select few the benefits are enormous: enhanced well-being, decreased homophobia, and that special sort of connection that comes between men who let their true selves be known to each other without fear of shame.

When I first became interested in the psychology of men I read a paper by William Pollack titled "No Man Is an Island" in which he identified the positive effects of emotional connections in men's lives.[1] Pollack's paper was rich in theory and research, and it was a real eye-opener for me. Still, something about the title kept nagging at me. One evening it eventually occurred to me: no man is an island, true, but many of us will spend a lifetime trying to find one. For people who find closeness in friendships to be a source of vitality and growth in their lives, this may seem like an odd notion. What could possibly be so attractive about living on a metaphorical island? In fact, there are many advantages. Consider the following:

> You are alone with your own thoughts, and there are no intrusions from others.
>
> You run no risk of being disappointed by other people.
>
> Any successes or failures are yours and yours alone.
>
> You are in total control of your own schedule.
>
> You spend more time dealing with the physical world than dealing with people.
>
> There are no relationship issues to deal with, and therefore fewer things to get upset about.

The great songwriter Chris Smither put a fine point on it in his insightful song "Help Me Now": "Every day is a solo played on a single string. Nobody shows up, nobody walks away". Later in the song, Smither astutely observes that "friends you don't make always let you be."

Many of the advantages of island living parallel the masculine norms I discussed in part I. Self-control, self-reliance, and emotional control are all much easier to accomplish in relative isolation from other people. At the same time, there are some serious disadvantages to island living:

Loneliness

No one to turn to for help if you need it

Boredom

Too much time to think

No "reality checks" from other people

Research on the role of social support in human relationships has produced very consistent findings. Supportive relationships with other people are associated with a wide range of physical and emotional benefits.[2–3] On average, women's friendships tend to be more emotionally supportive than men's and are characterized by greater levels of intimacy. However, as is always the case with research on gender differences, these are average findings. Not all men are the same, and some have friendships with other men that are very emotionally intimate.

One study by the psychologist Stephen Wester and his colleagues found that those men who tended to control their emotions, and those who were uncomfortable with physical affection between men, were the same men who experienced greater levels of psychological distress.[4] Interestingly, this link appeared to be due to lower levels of social support in these men's friendships.

Another study discovered that men with greater levels of social support in their relationships reported greater psychological growth following a highly stressful or traumatic event in their lives.[5]

Men's friendships are important not only because they provide potential sources of social support. Men also learn different behaviors from each other through the processes of modeling and social reinforcement. A man whose friends tend to engage in behaviors that promote well-being is himself more likely to do the same. In contrast, a man whose friends drink too much alcohol, make sexist comments about women, and fail to take care of their physical health is more likely to engage in similar behaviors.

## WHO ARE YOUR/HIS FRIENDS?

This is a good time for you to do some accurate self-assessment about the nature of your friendships. If you are a man, take a moment to consider who your close friends are. If you are a woman, you may do the same thing, or think about an important man in your life and complete the exercise as you imagine he might. It is helpful to begin by identifying which people in your life you would consider to be close friends. Consider a close friend someone with whom you feel a strong connection, someone who knows a good bit about your true inner life, and someone whom you would not hesitate to turn to for support in a difficult time. You might even jot down the names of people on a piece of paper.

Think about why you consider these people to be close friends. What's the first thing that comes to mind? Now take a few moments and think about the sorts of topics you discuss with your close friends. Try to identify those things that you talk about that you would not share with more casual friends or acquaintances. Another way to think about this is to ask yourself which parts of your true inner life you feel comfortable sharing with your close friends. Then consider what topics you would not feel comfortable discussing with your close friends. Finally, consider how often you talk with your close friends (every day, a few times a week, once a week, a few times a month).

Now take a few minutes to review your responses to this exercise. What do you notice? You might be surprised by how many, or how few, people you consider close friends. Or the numbers may have come out about how you expected. Everyone has expectations about the roles of friendships in their lives. Comparing the actual number of people you feel close to with what you expected can tell you several things. Perhaps you are someone who has fairly low expectations for closeness in friendships, and you also have relatively few close friends. Alternatively, you may be someone who would like more close relationships in your life. Or maybe you are someone who wants several close friendships and is fortunate enough to have them.

Next consider the things that make you feel close to your best friends. For some people it is primarily activities, and studies have shown that this may be especially true for men. For other people, both men and women, it is conversation that helps you feel close. Or perhaps it is an important shared experience in the past. Then think about how easy or difficult it was to come up with the topics that you feel comfortable or uncomfortable discussing with your close friends. This will tell you how clear you are, or how much thought you have given to what you can and can't talk about. Finally, look at how often on average you talk to your close friends. Any surprises there?

Most people find that when they take a close look at their friendships there are areas in which they would make changes if they could. The changes may be relatively small, or they may require some significant rethinking of what you expect from your friends and how you approach those relationships. There are many steps that men can take to improve the quality of their friendships. And there are many things that women can do to support men in these changes. The changes you might want to make will become much more apparent when you begin to understand the barriers many men face in developing close relationships with other men.

## FEAR AND FRIENDSHIP:
## THE CHALLENGES MEN FACE

Men's friendships with other men are typically characterized as hierarchical and action-oriented.[6] They are hierarchical because individual men are often exquisitely attuned to where they stand in relation to other men on a wide range of dimensions, including physical dominance, financial success, social status, and sexual fitness or prowess. Men's friendships are seen as action-oriented because they are typically more likely to engage in side-by-side as opposed to face-to-face sorts of interactions. Men are thought to enjoy doing things together, while women are more likely to enjoy talking for the sake of talking.

Being attuned to where they stand in a hierarchy and engaging in mutual activities can lead men to feel a certain type of closeness in friendships with other men. One of my oldest and closest friends, for example, told me after we had known each other for several years that when he first met me he went through a process of deciding whether I was a "worthy opponent." I knew exactly what he meant when he said it. Debating, ribbing each other, or playing golf or racquetball were all activities that allowed us to use the competition between us to bring us closer.

I once worked with a man who had very few close male friends.

At one point during our work together he made a new potential friend, and I asked him what he liked about this person. His response was telling: "I like this guy because we seem like equals. He has a Ph.D., but I make more money than he does. He's an excellent guitar player, but I got my M.B.A. from an Ivy League school." I could tell from his response that he felt a genuine affection for this man. Yet it also made me sad because the need to be equal on various scales of masculine accomplishment was such an immediate issue in the relationship. As I discussed in the previous chapter, intimacy between people, men or women, requires the presence of vulnerability. Not surprisingly, vulnerability and competition don't always go well together; when men feel vulnerable around other men they often hide it.

To understand men's friendships with other men, you must appreciate this fact: for many men, other men are as much a potential source of fear, shame, and betrayal as they are a potential source of companionship and support. This is the fundamental dilemma that men face. Becoming friends with another man is a risky prospect that raises many of the same long-standing conflicts regarding emotional intimacy that I discussed in the previous chapter. This fear is not always conscious and it may not be rational, but it is powerful and deeply rooted nonetheless. For most men it begins in childhood and continues to shape and influence their feelings about other men throughout their lives.

Are all men really that afraid of being rejected by other men? If so, how can we reconcile this with the fact that many men do develop close, trusting relationships in which they are able to let their guard down and reveal their true selves? Part of the answer comes from recognizing individual differences between men; some men are extremely image-conscious and deeply afraid of being shamed or called out by other men. And then there are men who are less affected by these fears. Nonetheless, from an early age all men are exposed to a social context with peers in which the threat of being ostracized, shamed, or otherwise emasculated by other males is ever present. Some boys and men navigate this dangerous ground by becoming relatively dominant in many of their social hierarchies. Others develop what the musician Tom Petty refers to as *rhino skin*, that tough exterior that lessens the pain of any potential injuries. And then some males are able to transcend the entire process and recognize it for what it is: a gendered social norm that restricts their well-being and the degree of intimacy and social support they can experience with and from other men.

The fear that men face in relating more intimately with other men is fueled by the wide range of gender norms that operate through *fear-based learning*. Fear-based learning is very common in humans and other living organisms. It occurs when we learn to do or not do certain things in order to *avoid* some form of punishment. Punishment is a very broad concept that extends beyond stereotypical parent-child or school-based forms of punishment, and includes any sort of consequence that people naturally prefer to avoid.

Children, for example, learn to avoid touching hot things because the behavior of touching such things has been followed by the punishment of getting burned. Humans are very adept at fear-based learning because they also have the advantage of using language to learn from the experiences of others without directly having to go through the exact same thing themselves. Continuing with the current example, many children never touch a hot stove, but they learn to avoid it anyway because their parents repeatedly say, "Stay away from that stove, it's hot!"

Fear-based learning also occurs in the context of complex

social situations where we develop and maintain relationships with others. The social world is full of potential punishers that range in severity from mild teasing to full-blown physical confrontation. Young children have been observed to use a wide range of punishers to influence each other's behavior and to communicate what sorts of thoughts, feelings, and actions are appropriate and inappropriate. One of the most common punishers young boys experience is being accused of being girly, gay, a mama's boy, a pussy, and so on.[7-8] These verbal accusations are often accompanied by other powerful social punishers such as being laughed at, pushed around, made fun of, and, perhaps most powerfully, excluded from the group. Young boys thus learn very quickly to do things that lead them to be perceived as appropriately masculine, and to avoid doing things that put them at risk of being perceived as feminine.

So far there is nothing particularly new about fear-based learning as a concept for understanding men's friendships; throughout this book I have emphasized the powerful roles that social reinforcers and punishers play in creating and maintaining silence and invisibility in men's lives. But there is an additional component to fear-based learning that makes it particularly salient in men's friendships. When organisms experience fear-based learning they learn to avoid not only the behaviors that preceded punishment but also the people, places, or situations that were associated with the punishment.

In his book *Coercion and Its Fallout*, the psychologist Murray Sidman describes many unfortunate consequences of fear-based learning, including excessive fear, anxiety, hypervigilance, and countercontrol, or the tendency for organisms to invest a great deal of energy in attempts to avoid being overly influenced by others.[9] To put it more colloquially, when others around us deliver punishing consequences, we learn to do our best to avoid not only those consequences but also the people who deliver them. This leaves many boys and men in a difficult spot when it comes to friendships with other men. *They desire closeness, connection, and support from the very same people who, throughout their lives, have been associated with delivering some of the most painful punishments.*

## THE MANY FACES OF FEAR IN MEN'S FRIENDSHIPS

So what is it exactly that men fear, and what makes these fears so powerful that they often render men silent and invisible around their male friends? Unfortunately, we can't simply ask men what they are afraid of because one of the first things males learn through fear-based learning is to deny fear. Boys who admit to being afraid of other boys are typically subject to additional shame and other forms of social rejection—never mind what initially led them to be afraid.

I recently asked a group of male undergraduate and graduate students if they had ever had experiences that led them to be afraid of other boys or men. They all looked at me as if I had asked them whether they had ever seen the sun rise—that's how obvious a question it seemed to them. Keep in mind that these were students enrolled in a fairly liberal university in New England. If anything, you might expect them to have had fewer such experiences because they were more likely to be outside the norms of mainstream American masculinity. Still, the stories they told revealed the many different ways boys and men can come to fear each other.

At the most basic level is the fear of being physically harmed. Virtually every adult man has a history of being the victim of a physical attack by another male at some point in his history. Many men have been attacked multiple times. Punches to the face, kicks in the testicles, assaults with weapons, and other forms of violence are all too common in the lives of young boys and teenagers. These experiences can leave a lasting sense of fear around other men that ranges from a mild sense of unease to outright phobia.

One student, Jim, told a story about his first year as a freshman on the high school soccer team. At the end of the first practice the coach told all the players that they would need to have a physical exam to keep playing. When the coach left, one of the older players turned to Jim and said, "Don't worry, I'll give you a physical out back, including a bum check." The other older players laughed knowingly. Jim was petrified and did his best to avoid being anywhere near the older players, so much so that he ultimately had to quit the team; the fear of being beaten, raped, or both, was so powerful it overtook his desire to play soccer and be part of a team.

Males also learn to fear being rejected by other men. Young boys quickly learn that your masculinity can be "called out" at any time. If it is called out, and you fail in any way to be perceived as masculine enough, you risk not only losing social status but perhaps losing friends as well. Even if you remain friends, there are powerful and painful emotions that go along with the experience of being publicly shamed, and which can leave a lasting sense of fear and anxiety around other men as an adult.

Another student, Mike, shared a story about his first serious sexual encounter with a girl. Things were awkward and didn't go as smoothly as he had hoped. Wanting to see if his experience was unusual, he confided in a friend, who told him not to worry, and things would get better. Then, a few days later, Mike was hanging out with his friend and a larger group of boys. The topic of sex came up, and Mike's friend proceeded to humiliate Mike by describing in detail Mike's failure to "get it up," "close the deal," and "be a man." All the boys laughed and added on a pile of insults at Mike's expense. Mike was so humiliated that he simply froze and endured the taunts, while vowing never again to be honest with another man about sexual experiences. As Mike said to our group, "It was just ultraclear to me. You can't trust guys to talk about stuff like that, even if they're close friends. You never know when they're going to use it to knock you down."

Mike's story points to another very common fear: betrayal by a close friend. If you put this fear together with the fact that many men never have more than a handful of close friends in their lives, it's easy to see how lasting the effects of such betrayals can be.

One student, Edward, told the story of finding his best friend in bed with his first real girlfriend when he was eighteen years old. Edward and his friend had grown up together throughout adolescence. They had confided many things to each other, including Edward's intense desire to have a girlfriend whom he loved. When Edward began dating this girl, he and his friend grew apart until the betrayal occurred.

Edward is now in his early thirties and still experiencing the aftereffects of this betrayal. "I guess I learned to never fully trust another guy around women I'm involved with; even with my wife, and we've been married for several years," he said. "I catch myself watching how my friends act around her, what they say to her, that sort of thing. It's a shame really because it's not like I actually think something is going to happen. But then there's that part of me where the fear is always lingering. What if I'm missing something?"

## A DIFFERENT KIND OF HOMOPHOBIA

Many people recognize the powerful effects of homophobia in men's relationships. *Homophobia* is typically understood as fear or hatred of homosexuals. Yet if you take the word apart, it translates roughly into "fear" (phobia) "of the same" (homo). This is partly why the sociologist Michael Kimmel suggests that homophobia is not necessarily limited to fear of homosexuality, although it may take that form at times.[10] From Kimmel's perspective, homophobia is best understood as a *general fear of other men*, and more specifically a fear of being shamed and accused by other men of being feminine or inadequately masculine. I sometimes use the term *fear of being femmed* to describe the general anxiety or homophobia that Kimmel describes.

It is worth repeating that homophobia, or the fear of being femmed, is not necessarily a fear of homosexuality. Kimmel points out that traditionally homophobic terms such as *queer* and *fag* are used by young boys even before they understand what homosexuality is. Boys use these terms to sanction other males who act, think, or feel in ways that are considered feminine. As a result, boys and men come to fear other men because any man is capable of calling into question their masculinity. This, Kimmel argues, is really what homophobia is all about.

So far we have considered the way homophobia manifests itself in fear of tangible consequences such as being physically assaulted, verbally humiliated, and so on. But homophobic fear can also have much more subtle effects in men's friendships. In these cases the fear is not of being perceived as gay or feminine, at least not directly, but of intimacy and vulnerability with another man. It is a fear of that unknown space of vulnerability between men where the possibility of being femmed exists.

One student, Mark, told a particularly moving story about the subtle role homophobia played in his relationship with a long-time friend named Sam. Mark and Sam had known each other since childhood. They held no secrets from each other and regularly looked forward to catching up on their lives. They spoke almost daily by phone despite the fact that they lived across the country from each other. About two years before Mark shared this story, Sam's mother passed away. Over the next few months they spoke less and less over the phone. Mark was concerned about Sam and wanted to reach out to him to find out how he was doing. But still the phone conversations remained fairly superficial. Mark began to feel awkward on the phone and started to avoid calling Sam. This led him to feel guilty about not reaching out more to his friend, and things got progressively worse from there.

When Mark recounted this story I was impressed by his honesty and vulnerability. Everyone in the room implicitly understood the difficulty of his situation and could empathize based on similar personal experiences with the pain and awkwardness of death. I asked Mark if he would mind discussing this issue further and trying to figure out, as a group, why it can be so hard to do something as seemingly simple as calling a friend and asking, "How are you really feeling?" It quickly became apparent that many of the fears we could all relate to were fears that reaching out in some way would make Mark vulnerable to a lack of response on Sam's part. For example, when Mark imagined calling up Sam and saying, "I've been concerned about you," he imagined Sam saying something like "Come on, now. Don't be a girl on me. You know I'm fine." Sam's imaginary response was one of femming Mark.

The group pushed further and began to unintentionally shame Mark by implying that he was not strong enough to endure such an obviously "irrational" fear and do the right thing by calling his friend. Mark made it clear that it was not just fear of being femmed directly. He identified the following fears as well:

- What if I get him so upset that he can't stop crying and we're stuck there dealing with all of that stuff for hours?

- What if I don't know what to say about such a delicate subject or I say the wrong thing?
- What if he tells me how angry he is that I haven't called sooner?
- What if I can't do anything to help him?

Mark's fears are about intimacy and emotional vulnerability with another man. They are fears of crossing the line into that area of unknown, unpredictable space where people are willing to let their real emotional lives be seen, while enduring the *possibility* that one or both of them will at some point be femmed.

## DUCKS ON THE WATER

You may have noticed that several of Mark's concerns seem more universally human than specific to men. Most people, for example, would have some level of concern about broaching a sensitive subject with a friend for fear of upsetting him or her. Yet the gender paradox remains; men's friendships seem, at least on the surface, to be quite different from women's.

What is happening on the surface versus what is going on below the surface is a crucial distinction when it comes to understanding men's friendships. When I think about the difference between how many men often act around their male friends, compared to what they may actually be experiencing privately, I am reminded of ducks on a pond. On the surface of the water everything appears to be ultrasmooth, but underneath everyone is paddling furiously to keep moving. Put another way, just because men are taught not to talk about the depth or complexity of their feelings about their friendships doesn't mean that such feelings don't exist. It simply means that they have run into additional forms of personal, private, and public silence. Because society discourages men from talking publicly about the strength of their emotions surrounding friendship, many men may have little or no experience identifying and describing their feelings about their male friends.

While women are expected and encouraged to "process" issues in their friendships, men are expected to take things in stride, not to make a big deal of things, not to expect too much, and so on. The resulting battle between the desire for intimacy with other men, on the one hand, and the pervasive homophobic threat of being femmed, on the other, leaves many men sensing few options when trying to improve the quality of their connections with other men.

One of the students in our research group told a story about a family member that poignantly illustrates just how different things can look on the surface compared to what is really going on inside when it comes to men's friendships.

Joe lived with his uncle, Steve, for a year during college. Steve was a talented auto mechanic and all-around handyman who was known among his friends for being both easygoing and always willing to lend a hand. When Joe was home with Steve the phone rang on a regular basis. Day and night Steve would get calls from friends asking if he could come and help them with a project. Steve always agreed and seemed to appreciate his friends' respect for the depth of his knowledge and his abilities.

Over time, Joe began to notice subtle signs that not every-thing was as it appeared on the surface. First Steve began to stop answering the phone as often and spent more time alone on nights and weekends. When he did answer the phone it was inevitably a friend or family member asking for his help. Steve would agree, but when he hung up the phone he would curse to himself or mutter as he walked out the door. At one point Joe overheard Steve saying to himself, "Would you be calling me so much if I didn't help you with your car?"

At this point in the story Joe paused and looked down. "What do you think was going on inside your uncle?" I asked. Joe's response revealed the depth of his empathy and compassion, and also the significant barriers he himself faced in reaching out to his uncle.

I felt really bad for him. I knew something had been bothering my uncle, but I didn't realize that he felt so taken advantage of. Actually, that was only part of it. I think he was starting to doubt whether his friends and family members really cared about him, or whether they just liked the idea of having a mechanic and handyman available on such short notice. I could tell that it really hurt, and I could also tell that he didn't want to talk about it. I felt totally stuck. I wanted to ask him how he was doing, and I wanted him to feel comfortable telling me what was going on. But at the same time I didn't want to embarrass him by pushing him to tell me what he was feeling. So I didn't say anything.

## HOW MEN CAN IMPROVE THEIR FRIENDSHIPS

There are many things men can do to improve the quality and/or quantity of their friendships. (For the things men's partners can do, see the next section.) Here are five suggestions that, collectively, will help men build better friendships.

### 1. NEVER UNDERESTIMATE THE PRESENCE OF FEAR

If you are a man, the premise that fear of other men affects all of your friendships may seem like an overstatement. After all, if you were so afraid of another man, why would you want to be friends with him? But before you reject the idea out of hand, remember that there are many different levels of fear. I am not suggesting that you fear for your physical safety around all other men. Fear can be as subtle as a looming sense of anxiety or unease; that nagging feeling that things aren't quite right or, if they are, that they could go wrong at any moment.

For most men, the fear that I am describing is not even conscious. Instead, it is a conditioned response that occurs almost like a reflex, the result of many years of social learning in which other males are always capable of femming them if the circumstances are right (or wrong, as it may be). By raising your awareness of how common this type of fear is you can begin to take control of it rather than letting it control you. One useful process is to identify the signs of fear, or even mild discomfort, around other men. Below are some common signs that, in combination, might indicate that you are experiencing the fear of being femmed.

- A desire to make yourself appear more masculine, successful, or powerful in the eyes of other men
- The desire to escape from an interaction
- The impulse to femme other men
- Physical signs such as muscle tension, headache, increased heart rate
- The impulse to dominate the conversation
- The impulse to make sexist comments or jokes
- Feelings of pressure to go along with the crowd even if their behavior makes you uncomfortable

## 2. IDENTIFY YOUR OWN THOUGHT PROCESSES
## WHEN YOU ARE AROUND OTHER MEN

In chapter 4, I discussed the power of our own thinking processes in determining how we act and feel. Thought processes can have a powerful effect in this regard when it comes to men's friendships. If you pay close attention, you will begin to notice the different thoughts that go through your mind when you are around other men. Imagine, for example, that you meet a guy with whom you have several interests in common. Eventually you think that you might like to pursue a friendship and see where it goes. You could invite this man out for coffee or perhaps to a sporting event. In the moment when extending an invitation first occurs to you, what thoughts go through your mind? Which thoughts will lead you to take steps toward pursuing a friendship, and which thoughts will lead you to avoid taking those steps? Can you imagine having any of the following thoughts?

> *It could be fun to spend some time with this person.*
> *He is probably going to think I'm desperate for friends.*
> *He will think I'm gay.*
> *What if this guy has a bunch of issues in his life that I don't want to know about?*
> *What if he turns out to be a jerk?*
> *Do I have room for a new friendship in my life?*
> *What if I ask him if he wants to get together, and he says no?*

## 3. ASSESS THE ACCURACY OF YOUR THOUGHTS

Once you know what you are thinking in a particular situation, you can assess the accuracy of your own thoughts. It is often helpful to ask yourself a series of questions: Are you making predictions of how things are going to go based on solid data? Or are you making inferences that are driven more by fear or uncertainty? Have you looked at the pros and cons of different courses of action? Have you asked yourself what the worst and best possible outcomes are? How likely is each of them to happen? If the worst happened, how bad would it actually be? Is it worth the risk?

## 4. SEE BELOW THE SURFACE AND DON'T BE FOOLED BY OTHER MEN

Most men are in the same boat when it comes to making and maintaining friendships; they want close relationships with other men but rarely if ever say so directly. As a result, most men look on the surface as if they are reasonably content with the status quo even though many of them share a great deal of discontent and longing on the inside. Under these circumstances it is all too easy for a man to wrongly conclude that he is different from other men, and that his desire for better friendships is somehow abnormal or embarrassing.

My friend Chris Kilmartin told me a story that illustrates just how easy it is for men to misread each other when they assume that another man's outward behavior is a good indicator of his inner life. Chris was working out at his local gym, riding the exercise bike and watching television, when another man walked up next to him, looked at the television, and said, "You think the Eagles have a chance this season?" Chris quickly concluded that this man was a "typical guy" who was interested only in sports. In order to avoid breaking any gender norms, and to get back to his workout as quickly as possible, Chris shrugged his shoulders and mumbled something like, "Who knows? I never get my hopes up." The other man nodded, sighed, and walked away.

Chris characterized this experience as "crazy." He explained: "Knowing nothing else about each other except for that brief interaction, we probably both came away assuming that the other guy was only into football and nothing else. He probably thought I was a 'typical guy.' You know, working out, watching a game. I know that's what I thought of him. He had no idea that I'm interested in the psychology of men, or that I do work on dating violence, or that I like to sing jazz standards. And I sure had no idea who he really was." I appreciate this story because it shows just how easy it is for two men to assume that the "other guy" is "different from me," when in fact they probably have much more in common than they realize. The take-home message is never to assume that a man's outward behavior reflects his true inner self, at least until you get to know him a bit.

## 5. TAKE CALCULATED RISKS

As your awareness of the nature of your friendships grows, you may find yourself wanting to make some changes. Perhaps you would like to have more friends. Or you might be interested in creating a stronger connection with some of your current friends. Change always involves risk, although the risk may not necessarily be a tangible one. It may be more emotional: the risk of being disappointed, the risk of failing, the risk of feeling hurt, and so on.

Risks are calculated when you have carefully considered the potential benefits against the potential losses. Just as with financial risks, there are individual differences in the degree to which people are willing to take emotional risks. Certain emotional risks have a relatively low probability of a fairly small bad thing happening, and a potential huge payoff on the other side. These are generally good risks to take when it comes to friendship.

For example, if you want to have a more meaningful connection with a friend, consider making your inner life seen and heard in ways that you haven't done previously. Rather than saying "Fine, nothing new" when a friend asks what's going on, try telling him what's actually going on, or at least part of it. If he seems surprised or doesn't respond well, give him a second chance. He may have been a little thrown by your willingness to be honest and direct. If you try again and he still seems unwilling or unable to handle it, at least you know something now about the type of friendship you can and cannot have with this person.

## HELPING WOMEN TO SEE MEN'S FRIENDSHIPS

Women are often surprised to learn of the depth of men's feelings about friendship. If you are a woman, you may know men who look very much like ducks on a pond when it comes to friendship; calmly gliding on the surface but paddling like hell below. By understanding both the complexity of men's feelings about friendship, and also their reluctance to talk about their friends in stereotypically emotional terms, you may begin to realize just how difficult it is for many men to establish intimate friendships with other men.

To empathize with men's struggles regarding friendship is to allow men to feel understood and respected. Empathy need not be a long, drawn-out process of verbally dissecting the nuances of a man's relationship with his friends. In fact, some men may find that very process shameful and feminizing. Remember that just because a man has powerful feelings about friendship does not mean that he is necessarily able to put words to them. If you are someone who finds it fairly easy to put words to your feelings, you may naturally gravitate in this direction when trying to empathize with a man about his friendships. If you find that this does not work well, try using fewer words. A simple "I know your friendship with Mark isn't always what you want it to be" can go a long way toward letting him know that you understand.

You can also learn quite a bit about the quality of a man's friendships by paying attention to how he looks and acts just before and after seeing his friends. Does he look forward to seeing them, or does it seem to be more of a habit? Does he put effort into getting together with them, or does he rely only on established times such as a regular golf game or other event? When things are particularly stressful at work or at home, does he make extra efforts to meet with friends, or does he withdraw from them? How does he behave after getting together with friends? Does he seem energized? Or does he seem more irritable or disappointed?

If you pay close attention and you begin to wonder about how his friendships are going, you might try talking to him about it. As I suggested in the previous chapter, keep this sort of conversation relatively short and casual to start.

You might begin with something like "How's it going with your friends these days?" If his response suggests that he finds the question threatening ("What do you mean, 'how's it going?' It's fine"), drop the subject. Then try following up a couple of days later. Rather than asking questions, make a short and honest statement about your own concerns. For example, you might say, "I don't want to put you on the spot, but I want you to know that I've been wondering how things are going with Steve. You don't seem as interested in getting together with him as you used to. Let me know if you ever want to talk about it."

If he insists that everything is fine and you are overanalyzing things, don't argue with him. Remember, most men have been taught that having strong feelings about friendships with other men is not particularly manly. To admit disappointment, fear, love, or a desire for greater closeness with other men is to admit your own needs for human connection. For many men, to admit this very basic human need is to make yourself extremely vulnerable by admitting that, in fact, you cannot and do not want to live on an island.

## SUMMARY

Traditional notions of manhood make it difficult for men to establish close, intimate friendships with other men. At the same time, many men sense that there is something lacking in their friendships and long for more meaningful connections. Most of the barriers men face in deepening their friendships are based on fear of other men; in particular, the fear that other men can call their masculinity into question at any time. Expressing the desire for closeness, initiating a friendship, or revealing something personal about a man's own vulnerabilities are all potential risks for being shamed or otherwise rejected by other men.

Men can overcome many of these barriers by taking stock of the quality and quantity of their current friendships and deciding whether any changes are warranted. Changes are easier to make, and have a higher likelihood of success, if men assess their own thoughts about friendship with other men, determine the accuracy of those thoughts, and take calculated risks within new and existing friendships.

Women can do their part to enhance their empathy for men's struggles with friendships. The first step is recognizing that even though men may not talk openly about the complexities of their friendships, most men have strong feelings about them. Although some men may not be open to discussing these feelings at length, women can still communicate their respect for and understanding of the challenges men face when establishing and maintaining close friendships with other men.

# PART III

---

# STAYING SEEN AND HEARD

# 8

# Coping with Stressful Life Events

It is remarkable how much of what we do on a daily basis occurs outside of our immediate awareness. Much like a long road trip in which we automatically steer the car, life settles into a rhythm. Every once in a while we wake up when new challenges arise. When it comes to driving a car, maybe traffic is slowing, or maybe we become bored because there's nothing good on the radio. When it comes to life, perhaps our usual approach to coping is no longer working for us. In either case, we have to figure out what to do about the situation we find ourselves in, and this requires conscious change.

The death of a loved one, a change in employment status, physical illness, divorce, or the birth of a child—these are just a handful of the stressful life events that can challenge us. Life stress also tends to draw us all into familiar ways of coping with problems, regardless of how effective they are. I once worked with a man who had an extensive history of substance abuse, including alcohol, marijuana, cocaine, and heroin. He had been sober for twelve years at the time of our meeting, and he expressed no desire to return to his previous lifestyle.

Nonetheless, when he lost his job, the familiar cravings came back and he fell off the wagon a couple of times. His wife first became afraid and then angry at his apparent lack of willpower. The more stressed his marriage became, the stronger his cravings grew.

A similar pattern can occur with men's silence and invisibility. If a man tends to keep to himself, to handle all of his problems on his own, and to avoid experiencing his own distress as much as possible, these tendencies will become even stronger during periods of increased stress.

Psychologists have ranked the power of different stressful life events. As it turns out, many of the most stressful ones are those that are most challenging for men to navigate while staying silent and invisible. These include divorce, unemployment, physical illness, and death of a loved one.

## DIVORCE

Rates of divorce steadily increased throughout the twentieth century and have remained relatively stable since the 1970s. Approximately one half of all first marriages will end in divorce. The rates are even higher for second and third marriages.[1] Yet despite how common it is, divorce still carries with it a good amount of social stigma. Divorced people face many challenges: remaining connected to friends and family, wrestling with financial stresses, promoting positive development in their children, and forming new relationships.

Divorce can be highly stressful for all individuals, but men, and particularly men who are emotionally and socially isolated, can face substantial challenges. Consider the following. Women are twice as likely as men to initiate divorce, and this means that men are twice as likely as women to be the "dumpee" rather than the "dumper." Men typically have fewer friends, extended family, and other forms of social support to help cope with divorce.[2-3] This fact, combined with many men's tendency to keep their pain and suffering to themselves, means that they must work extra hard during and after divorce to remain connected to a social network. This may help explain why men are much quicker than women to remarry following divorce. Finally, the consistently higher rates of anger and substance abuse among men suggest that they may be at a higher risk for developing or relapsing into such problems when divorce does occur.

These problems may be attempts at self-medication; one Canadian study found that men who had divorced or separated were six times more likely to report an episode of depression compared with the men who remained married. In contrast, women who had split up with their spouse were only three and a half times more likely to have experienced depression compared to still-married women. A more recent study discovered that divorced or separated men were two and a half times more likely to commit suicide than married men.[4-5]

In addition to the general stress caused by divorce, there are more specific and powerful emotions that some men experience, and which many of them choose to keep to themselves. To begin with, divorce entails the loss of roles that are central to many men's identities. If children are involved, men may feel a strong sense of loss in their role as a parent. Many custody arrangements result in men seeing their children less often than when they were married. The common pattern of dividing up friends, as well as the potential loss of in-law relationships, can also contribute to men's loss of identity as a friend and family member.

Earlier we considered the education young boys receive in how to cope with the loss of close relationships. Beginning with societal, familial, and peer pressures to separate from their mothers, boys learn that the grief they feel at the loss of close relationships is shameful and should be kept to oneself. In effect, the message is that it is more important to prevent yourself from being seen as emotionally dependent than it is to allow yourself to actually experience the loss. As a result, many adult men are woefully unprepared to cope with the array of strong feelings they encounter when getting divorced. Instead, men are expected to "move on," "put it behind you," "get back in the game," and so on.

The problem, of course, is that divorce is typically an immense loss, no matter how amicable or conflict-ridden the process is. Losses require some grieving in order to move through them adaptively and continue on with life. Refusing to feel what you feel, staying silent or hidden, or channeling all your vulnerable emotions into anger can prevent the natural grieving process.

## JOB LOSS

Given the current economic climate worldwide, unemployment and job loss are critical issues for many women and men. The personal economic challenges of these transitions have been known for some time. Unemployment is associated with a wide range of social, emotional, and physical problems.[6-7] In the United States the gradual erosion of the middle class over the last several decades has raised the stakes even higher.

The notion that a successful masculine identity is dependent on being a breadwinner is centuries old and shows little sign of changing. Despite the fact that women are increasingly competitive in the marketplace, and men face historically unprecedented opportunities to redefine their sense of self in the work-life balance, many men continue to feel a loss of identity, self-esteem, and self-efficacy when they are faced with unemployment.

Patrick, whose story I told in the prologue, is a good example of a man who found the collapse of his own business so painful that he came close to taking his own life. Like many men in similar situations, Patrick chose to keep his shame and uncertainty silent and invisible. As a result, no one, not even his closest friends and family, knew what was going on.

As with divorce, many men feel the effects of job loss in deep and personal ways that may never see the light of day. The recent rise in numbers of documented suicide-homicides among men is one dramatic example of this; many of these men cite work-related stress or job loss as critical factors in their decision to take their own lives and those of their family members.

But the effects of silent and invisible suffering following the loss of a job need not be this dramatic in order to leave powerful reverberating effects in the lives of men and their friends and families. Depression, substance abuse, and anger are common outcomes when men are unable or unwilling to find sources of social and emotional support. Some men may be at more risk than others. Those who place a great deal of emphasis on their jobs as a source of identity and self-pride may be more likely to suffer psychological effects as well as economic hardships as a result of unemployment. Men whose social networks revolve primarily around work may also experience a double loss; in addition to the loss of income and professional identity, these men may find themselves increasingly isolated from others in general.

Finally, personal feelings of shame, inadequacy, guilt, and fear may be particularly difficult to work through for men who stay silent and invisible following the loss of their jobs. While a graduate student at Clark University, MySha Whorley conducted her dissertation research on the psychological effects of unemployment in men. She found that many men who had recently lost their jobs were reluctant to discuss their experiences with friends or family because of shame, embarrassment, and guilt. As part of her research, MySha gave these men the opportunity to spend up to twenty minutes writing a letter to someone close to them describing their thoughts and feelings about unemployment. Those men who wrote reported benefiting greatly from the experience, and at a three-month follow-up, they were experiencing lower levels of shame and depression.

## ILLNESS

Major physical illnesses can lead even the most emotionally open of individuals to retreat inward. For men who already tend to go in that direction, a chronic or acute medical condition provides all the more reason to go underground. This may seem counterintuitive since social support during times of illness can be a major asset when a person is vulnerable. Yet if you consider the power of masculine norms like self-reliance, physical strength, and emotional control, you can begin to see how hiding when you are ill makes a certain amount of sense. If an illness necessarily makes you dependent on others, you may fear losing your self-reliance. If it weakens you, you are less powerful and strong than usual. And if it creates strong emotions like fear, anger, grief, and despair, it is that much harder to control your emotions. In short, physical illnesses are capable of robbing men of their sense of their own manhood. As a result, feeling weak, dependent, and emotional is, for many men, precisely the time to hide from others.

Other men go underground when they become ill not because they are ashamed of their own vulnerability but because they are experiencing a great deal of fear and have no way to express it. Fear in general is dangerous territory for many men since traditional masculine norms punish men for experiencing or expressing it. But there is more to it than the general fear of fear. For many of the reasons I considered in chapter 4, physical vulnerability, such as that which comes with serious illness, is particularly threatening for many men. Some have had little or no experience with the health care system following traumatic experiences in youth. Remember the carpenter who as a child suffered extreme pain in silence when a doctor probed the bone of his chin with a scalpel. Such experiences can easily result in men fearing vulnerability and dependence on a physician even more than they fear the potential consequences of not seeking help.

Traditional masculine norms can also create powerful fear of a man's own mortality. The truly masculine body, men are told, is immune to any sorts of serious problems, real men are expected to overcome physical ailments through sheer willpower. This includes such expectations as playing through the pain, gutting it out, and so on. Many women, in contrast, are socialized from a young age to expect their bodies to be vulnerable and to regularly practice self-care, as well as seeking help from health care professionals. Books such as *Our Bodies, Ourselves* and the expectation of annual gynecological checkups are two examples in this regard. Many men, on the other hand, are woefully inexperienced when it comes to confronting physical illnesses and distinguishing the difference between what is a treatable problem and what may actually be fatal. As a result, these men often fear the worst when they become aware that something may truly be wrong.

For all of these reasons, the possibility of a serious physical illness is enough to drive many men underground at precisely the time when they need to reach out to friends, family members, and health care professionals. I had my own personal run-in with this dynamic several years ago, when I was misdiagnosed with multiple sclerosis. For six months I lived with the belief that I was suffering from a progressive, degenerative neurological disorder. Despite all of my background in the psychology of men, as well as the knowledge that many people with MS lead long, productive lives, my day-to-day life was governed by a virtually incapacitating fear that I would die (or forever lead a life of debilitation and despair) and by the impulse to hide from those who loved and cared about me.

I was fortunate that the diagnosis was incorrect, and my symptoms were surgically corrected following discovery of bone spurs on my cervical vertebrae. And in an odd way, I feel fortunate to have experienced what it is like to be simultaneously deeply afraid, ashamed of my own fear, and compelled to hide it from others. I believe it greatly enhanced my ability to empathize with men in similar situations.

## DEATH OF A LOVED ONE

The death of a loved one, be it a child, parent, sibling, or close friend, can be extremely painful for all of us. For some men it can be debilitating not only because the loss itself is painful but also because they are unprepared for the experience of intense grieving, combined with shame and embarrassment about their own powerful needs for connection. Like divorce, the death of a loved one forces men to confront their own very basic needs for connection, security, and emotional intimacy with others. If a man feels ashamed of such needs, as many men do, the grieving process can become complicated or unresolved.

Men's friendships, family relationships, and intimate relationships all play a role in shaping how the grieving process unfolds. If a man tends toward the silent and invisible, he is more likely to have friends and family members who expect him to continue in that role. This expectation can also complicate the grieving process by restricting opportunities to share the loss. Because the death of a loved one can be a risky time for many men, it is especially important that these men, and those who love them, do whatever they can to allow the pain to be seen and heard.

## HOW TO STAY SEEN AND HEARD

Staying seen and heard through difficult times is not unlike staying clean and sober once a person has made the commitment to change his or her ways. The first step is recognizing that old habits die hard. For men who have developed a lifelong pattern of keeping their inner lives hidden, it can be tremendously difficult to open up when the stakes seem that much higher. Empathy, both from oneself and from others, can be very helpful in this regard. Criticism, on the other hand, is more likely to lead to shame, defensiveness, and anger. Simply recognizing that it is hard to open up during stressful times can help men to do precisely that.

The second step is to do whatever you can to avoid slipping back into old patterns. For men, this may mean making conscious efforts to act counter to their natural inclinations. For those close to men, it may mean avoiding the pressure to slip back into ignoring what is really going on. This can be difficult, since being silent and invisible, and failing to see and hear another person, are reciprocal processes; the more men obscure their inner lives, the easier it is to conclude that there is not much there to see or hear.

During times of transition and stress this is a serious mistake and can lead to many of the significant problems we have considered throughout this book.

The third step is to make sure that you continue the process of sober self-assessment I described in chapter 3. If you are a man, take stock of your situation by asking yourself the following questions:

Have recent events in my life led me to go (back) underground?

What sorts of thoughts and emotions am I keeping from myself or from others close to me?

Am I behaving in ways that might be keeping my true self silent and invisible?

If so, what are they, and what are the consequences for me, and for others?

Is my current approach to handling my private inner life consistent with my personal values and goals?

If you are a woman, or someone concerned about a man you are close to, many of the same questions will be relevant—with one exception. Rather than focusing on your own inner life, consider how your own thoughts, emotions, and behaviors are impacting the man you are concerned about.

The next step involves taking some calculated risks. Ask yourself what the potential gains and losses are of sharing what's going on in your life with others. Or, if you are concerned about a particular invisible man in your life, consider the pros and cons of encouraging him to open up. The potential changes you consider need not be monumental. It may be as simple as expressing your concern directly. Or, if you are the person others are concerned about, it may be a matter of making parts of yourself more audible and visible.

A couple of years ago I was reminded of the payoffs that can come from taking calculated risks when I had a conversation with, of all people, the pizza guy. Everybody knows the pizza guy. He comes to your house, you give him the money, and he gives you the pizza. That's the extent of your relationship. You might exchange a "How's it going?" and a "Fine, how about you?" or you might comment on the weather, and that's really all that's called for. But one winter evening in 2008 I had had a particularly stressful day at work and was thinking about it when the doorbell rang. When I opened the door to the pizza guy, he greeted me with "Hi, how's it going?" Normally, I would say, "Good, how about you?" But this time, something clicked inside me. How was it really going? Actually, it wasn't going that well. Not only was I angry about a situation at work, but I was also worried about a relative's health. And an old injury had been nagging at me for several days. For whatever reason, I decided to be honest. The conversation then went like this:

"Well, I've had better days. This one has been a struggle," I said. I didn't say it with that "life is life" tone of voice that essentially says, "Things are tough, but don't ask me any more about it. I've got it under control." Instead, I looked at him directly and stated honestly that, in fact, at this particular time, I was not doing so well. He looked me in the eyes and was silent for a moment. I could tell that he was surprised by my response. Then he looked down and said, "I know what you mean. My grandmother died yesterday."

Now it was my turn to be shocked. I could not believe that this man with whom previously I had exchanged nothing but the most cursory greetings would feel comfortable telling me such a powerful thing about his life. I immediately felt closer to him, and I could *see* the pain he was in. "I'm so sorry to hear that," I said. "How are you doing?"

> PIZZA GUY:  It's tough. My mother is very upset, and so are my brothers and sisters.
>
> ME:  Are you all there for each other?
>
> PIZZA GUY:  Yeah. We talk, but it's still really sad.
>
> ME:  I was very young when my grandmother died. My family didn't talk about it much.
>
> PIZZA GUY:  Yeah. It's tough right now.
>
> ME:  I really wish you and your family the best. I'm very sorry that you lost your grandmother.

I paid him, and he handed me the pizza. Then he took a couple of steps down the walkway and paused. He turned and looked at me and said, "Thanks for talking."

"Thank you," I said. "Thank you for telling me about your grandmother."

Three things stand out to me about this experience. First, we never would have broached the subject of his grandmother if I had not been willing to admit to myself, and to the pizza guy, that I was struggling that day. In other words, my own willingness to take a chance allowed someone else to open up. I wonder how often men miss an opportunity to connect with each other because of their own unwillingness to make themselves the least bit vulnerable.

The second thing to note is that our interaction was relatively brief. We didn't stand there for hours pouring out our hearts and souls to each other. The entire conversation could not have taken more than a couple of minutes. Sometimes this is all it takes.

Most men do not want to go over and over their feelings about issues in their lives. But most men want to be heard, and to be seen as real people facing real issues. Taking a couple of minutes to honestly share what's happening in your life can be tremendously liberating.

Third, I was struck by the particular way we communicated with each other. There was not a lot of "feeling" talk. No one said, "I'm torn up on the inside," "I feel deeply sad," or anything like that. There is nothing wrong with such feeling words. In fact, they can be quite helpful in articulating what's happening inside you. But for many men these types of words simply are not necessary to describe personal or private experiences. For the pizza guy and me, at that particular moment, it was enough to say that things were "tough" and that we were "sorry."

Unfortunately, no sooner had I taken a calculated risk by opening up to another man than I shot myself in the foot in a matter of minutes. (I suspect that I am not alone in this and that many men have had similar experiences.)

The restaurant where the pizza guy worked was a favorite of mine. I especially enjoyed the steak and cheese sub with grilled onions, tomatoes, hot peppers, mushrooms, and provolone cheese. This sandwich was a well-loved and regular part of my life for several years. And also for several years, the sandwich often arrived missing anywhere from two to three of the key ingredients. On this particular night, I tore open the white paper wrapping to find that the sandwich was missing the hot peppers, mushrooms, onions, and tomatoes. I was staring in disbelief at a steak and cheese sub with none of my favorite accompanying ingredients.

My first reaction was disappointment, but that didn't last long. Men are not supposed to feel disappointed. It's too vulnerable a position to be in. So instead I started to get angry. *Why does this happen, again and again? Why are they taking advantage of me?* In my head the situation began to revolve around dominance. I happened to know that the head chef was a man, and I started to develop the sense that he was doing something to put me in a "one-down" position. He was taking advantage of me repeatedly. Relatively quickly I got it in my head that this was "not right!"

*It's not OK that he does this all the time,* I kept telling myself. Of course, it's not OK to not get what you pay for on a regular basis. But this was about more than that. It was about having the sense that I was being taken advantage of, and for many men this is simply an unacceptable feeling.

I decided to call the guy and try to calmly tell him what had happened. Here is how the interaction went.

> ME: Hello, this is Michael Addis. I ordered some food a little while ago. I ordered a steak sub with grilled onions, mushrooms, hot peppers, tomatoes, and provolone. The thing is, the sandwich came without the hot peppers, mushrooms, onions, or tomatoes. And I have to admit, this isn't the first time this has happened.
>
> HEAD CHEF: Well, I made that sandwich, and I know what I put on it. I put all those things on it.

Now the air was really starting to thicken with masculinity. I had apparently come across as critical, and the chef was getting defensive. The problem was, I heard his response as if he was saying, "There's something wrong with you and your ability to judge the contents of a sandwich." It sounds ridiculous even as I write this. But if you're a man, you've undoubtedly been in a similar situation. If you're a woman, ask a man you know to read my account of this interaction and see what he thinks. The need to be right can easily supplant all other needs and dominate an interaction with another man.

As I said, things were now beginning to heat up because both of us were feeling criticized and our sandwich assessment abilities were being questioned. The conversation continued:

ME: Well, I'm sitting here looking at the sandwich, and I don't see any of those things.

HEAD CHEF: I don't know what to tell you, buddy. I know what I put in the sandwich.

ME: I guess we have a problem [an astute observation from a trained clinical psychologist]. Believe me, I would rather be sitting down and enjoying this sandwich rather than debating with you about what's in it. But please believe me, none of those things came in the sandwich.

HEAD CHEF: Look, Mister, I make sandwiches all day long. I know what I do and don't put in them, so I don't know what to tell you.

ME: Look, I have two eyes in my head, and I know what I do and don't see. I don't want to argue with you, but if you're not going to take my word for it, I'll just need to take my business elsewhere.

HEAD CHEF: You're welcome to do that.

ME: OK, that's what I'll do.

Then I hung up the phone. Boy, was that productive!

I bring up this example for several reasons. First, it illustrates how stubbornness, competitiveness, and the need to be right can detract from a man's quality of life. The fact is that I liked having food delivered from this restaurant, and I can no longer enjoy that option. After all, the chef might do something to my food! I say this only half jokingly. When men fight, there is always the fear of retaliation at some point in the future.

This example also illustrates well how masculinity can be in the air between men. As far as I know, I don't possess a sandwich assessment gene that causes me to lash out whenever hot peppers or grilled onions are missing. And I also don't seem to have a set of hypermasculine personality traits that causes me to have daily arguments with other men. Rather, like all people, I inherited a certain sensitivity to being cheated. And my personality is such that I am more or less competitive, or argumentative, depending on the situation. When, for whatever reason, all of the ingredients come together—my genetic inheritance, my personality style, *and* a particular series of events in my environment—masculinity is in the air.

Finally, this is a good example of how easy it is to slip back into old patterns. I had taken a risk by sharing a small part of my life with the pizza guy, and the gamble had paid off. But for that one step forward, I quickly took two steps back by becoming argumentative, defensive, and accusatory. Apparently, I was more comfortable expressing hard emotions outwardly than I was dealing with what was really going on. And here's the part of this that is the hardest to admit: I was far more pained by my subsequent interaction with the chef than I was by my initial disappointment over the sandwich. At the time, the pain was effectively buried under several layers of anger, indignation, and self-righteousness. But it was there. This is a truth that many men either are unable to admit or are simply unaware of. When we feel one-upped, when we get angry, and our defenses go up, we are hurting privately. And the hurt doesn't always go away. We can brood over these sorts of interactions. And underneath the anger, resentment, frustration, and self-righteous indignation is a lingering sense of having been wounded. Wounds hurt. That's a fact of life.

Perhaps it does not matter that this type of hurt remains silent and invisible. After all, it's not as if I had lost a loved one in a car accident. I simply had an argument with the chef of a pizza parlor. On the other hand, if you consider the consequences of my inability or unwillingness to acknowledge that I was, in fact, hurting, I believe that this sort of silence does matter. Here are some of those consequences:

- Loss of one option for having food delivered
- Loss of enjoyment of the time spent sitting and eating dinner, as opposed to time spent arguing on the phone
- Poor modeling for my daughter of how to handle disappointment
- Shame and embarrassment at having gotten myself into such a situation

## WHEN HELP IS NO LONGER A FOUR-LETTER WORD

At the beginning of this book I told the story of Patrick, who came very close to taking his own life rather than sharing his problems with family members, friends, or a professional. As it turned out, my experience with Patrick was a turning point for me and set into motion my interest in men's mental health. I found Patrick's case compelling for many reasons. To begin with, I had spent six years prior to meeting Patrick, and several years after, conducting research on the process and outcome of mental health treatments for depression and anxiety disorders. My own research, and that of many others over a period of several decades, seemed to lead to three consistent findings.

First, both talk therapies and medications turn out to be effective treatments for these problems. Second, the overwhelming majority of people suffering from these problems never receive treatment from a professional. Third, and most distressing to me, men are far less likely than women to seek treatment, and of those who make it to treatment, men are far more likely to drop out prematurely.[8]

The data on men and mental health services were both unsurprising and deeply disturbing. I could not stop myself from asking, again and again: if there are effective treatments available, why are men so reluctant to use them? This was all the more troubling because I was raised in a family where help was anything but a four-letter word. My parents both worked in the mental health field, and while growing up I was always encouraged to talk about my feelings with friends, family, and, when necessary, with a counselor. I benefited so much from this encouragement that it struck me as tragic and mystifying that more men would not have had similar experiences.

Now, after close to a decade of exploring this question, I am less mystified and my empathy for men's struggles in seeking help has increased quite a bit. It comes down to this: if you have been encouraged all of your life to keep your emotions under control, to handle problems on your own, and to avoid making yourself vulnerable to others, particularly other men, probably the last thing you want to do when life gets difficult is discuss your most private thoughts and feelings with a stranger. I thus find myself in a somewhat curious position. I am an advocate for men using mental health services, while recognizing and accepting that doing so can be enormously difficult for some men—especially when life is already throwing them curveballs and their confidence and self-esteem are shaken.

I therefore spend a good deal of my time talking to both men and women about the conditions under which it makes sense for a man to seek help from a professional. The first thing to consider is that, except under the most severe circumstances, there are no hard-and-fast rules. By *severe*, I mean situations in which a man is experiencing so much stress and unhappiness that he is at serious risk of harming himself or another person. Under these circumstances, seeking professional help is always warranted. If a man refuses, it is appropriate to enlist the help of friends or family members to develop a plan for gently confronting him and expressing your concern. He may temporarily feel betrayed, and may be angry at having apparently lost control of his own situation. However, emergency situations require quick and direct action. When such steps are taken out of love and compassion they rarely leave lasting negative effects.

More typical is a situation in which a man and those who love him know that he is struggling, but it is unclear whether it is appropriate to seek professional help. In such a case it is helpful to consider the following questions:

For how long have the problems or symptoms been occurring?

How much distress are they causing for the man and/or those around him?

How much are they interfering with his day-to-day functioning at work, school, or in the family?

What steps have been taken to deal with the issues on his own, and how effective have they been?

Keep in mind that some men may not be in the best position to answer for themselves, simply because they are not used to paying attention to their own emotional well-being. In these cases, getting the additional perspective of a partner, close friend, or family member can be very helpful.

Also bear in mind that talk therapies and medication are not the only effective ways to overcome depression, anxiety, existential issues, or relationship problems. Self-help (e.g., books, Internet resources), exercise, and increasing social support through talking with friends and family have all been found to be helpful.[9–11] Unfortunately, many men see turning to others and helping oneself as mutually exclusive options.

In fact, nothing could be farther from the truth. Turning to others is a form of helping oneself, and no one can make the choice to do so but the person suffering. Moreover, for many people, disclosing their real selves to others requires tremendous courage and self-discipline. For many men, in particular, talking to others is anything but "giving up," "copping out," or "being dependent." Rather, it is a courageous first step in taking control over their own situation. Finally, talking with others often leads to new ideas for how to improve your own situation. After twenty-five years in this field I have never seen, nor heard of, a successful case of therapy that did not involve a person making his or her own self-directed changes in how to approach life. Every therapist or counselor knows it is the clients who do the work that produces lasting change.

## MISCONCEPTIONS ABOUT MEDICATION

In my research with my colleagues we have found that many men have negative reactions to the prospect of taking medication for such problems as depression and anxiety. Some of these men have had bad experiences with medication in the past, and I can certainly understand their reluctance. But many of the men we have interviewed also have strong negative views based on misunderstandings fueled by myths about psychotropic medications. At the risk of sounding like a zealous advocate for medication, which I most certainly am not, I am going to debunk some common myths about medication. I do so in the hope that women and men reading this book can make informed decisions about their options without being constrained by popular misconceptions.

- *Myth: Medications are addictive.*
  Fact: Most psychotropic medications (e.g., antidepressants) are not addictive because they do not produce any sort of immediate effect that could make a person crave more and more. The one exception is fast-acting medication, such as Valium or Xanax. Medications such as Zoloft and Prozac work very slowly to readjust how your nervous system operates. Thus they are not addictive in the way that street drugs and fast-acting anxiety medications can be.
- *Myth: Medications will change my personality and turn me into someone I'm really not.*
  Fact: There is no evidence that medications change a person's personality. Our personalities are the result of many complex interactions involving our minds, our bodies, our current environments, and the ways we were raised. Typically, no single factor can take over and change who we are.
- *Myth: Taking medications is a cop-out because I've given up handling the situation on my own.*
  Fact: Taking medication is one way to begin handling a situation on your own. Medications by themselves do not absolve a person from the need to make changes. Instead, they often help a person to take important action.

- *Myth: Once I begin taking medication I will have to be on it for the rest of my life.*

  Fact: Most prescribing physicians suggest a course of at least six months on medication, but after that, whether you continue depends on how well you are feeling, what's going on in your life, and other personal factors that will influence your decision.

- *Myth: If I tried medication and it didn't help, it isn't going to help in the future.*

  Fact: Many people never give their first attempt with medication a fair trial. Modern medications often take two to three weeks to begin helping. Sometimes, for unknown reasons, some medications work better than others for different people. Thus, rather than giving up completely, it often makes sense to try a different medication if the first one is not effective.

## HOW TO SEEK PROFESSIONAL HELP

One of the reasons more people do not receive effective help from mental health care professionals is that it can be hard to find one. Simply flipping through the Yellow Pages is not particularly useful since many people don't know the difference between a counselor, a psychologist, a psychiatrist, and a social worker. More important, knowing a professional's degree does not tell you much about what that person would be like to work with, whether the two of you will click, and so on. Here are a few suggestions for how to go about seeking professional help.

- Seek a referral from a trusted source. This could be a friend, a family member, your primary care physician or family doctor, or an employee assistance program.

- Commit to at least one visit. People are sometimes put off by being put on hold when calling for an appointment, by a brusque receptionist at the office, or by or other initial obstacles. Try to reserve judgment until you actually meet with a professional.

- Pay attention to how comfortable you feel with the person, while recognizing that your discomfort may have less to do with the person as an individual and more to do with the awkwardness of a new situation. Above all, mental health professionals should have excellent people skills. You should feel that you are being listened to, that the person cares about your situation and is confident about being able help you. If you don't click with the person, you are under no obligation to continue seeing him or her. Try someone else and see if it feels any different.

- Pay attention to how you are interpreting the meaning of seeking help, or how you are communicating with a loved one about the prospect of seeking help. Rather than seeing it as giving up or copping out, try seeing it as getting some consultation, extra coaching, or a more objective point of view on your situation. Remember that if we take away the stigma associated with mental health care, what we're really talking about is getting some additional coaching or feedback on an individual's emotional well-being. In principle, there is nothing different about this than getting a physical checkup, taking your car to a mechanic, or any other situation where professional input can help you to solve problems that you can't handle entirely on your own. There is no shame in that.

## SUMMARY

Once men begin to make their inner lives audible and visible, stressful events can be risk factors for going back underground.

Some of the most common stressful events include the death of a loved one, unemployment, divorce, and physical illness. Sober self-assessment is crucial during these times. Men should take honest stock of how they are feeling privately and the quality of their personal relationships. Partners, friends, and family members should be aware that stressful events can lead men to shut down quickly and turn inward. Reaching out at such times can be very beneficial.

There is no shame in seeking professional help to get feedback or a fresh perspective on a man's life situation. Unfortunately, the stigma that often surrounds masculinity and mental health has created numerous obstacles for men when they consider the possibility of seeking help. Some obstacles take the form of myths about medication and/or therapy. Others are more tangible and have to do with lack of knowledge about how to seek help or what to expect from an initial meeting with a professional. It takes courage and perseverance to seek help, and the payoffs can be positive and substantial. Research shows that both talk therapies and medications can be very helpful when people are struggling with depression, anxiety, or related issues.

# 9

# Societal Change

Much of this book has been about the lives of individual men, women, and children. Yet the challenge of men's silence and invisibility extends far beyond the issues we all face in our individual lives. In this final chapter I will address several larger scale factors that must be attended to if we are to make substantial progress in rendering men's lives more visible and audible.

## BEYOND INDIVIDUALS: SOCIAL HEALTH

Most contemporary scientists who study human behavior recognize that almost all of our experiences are simultaneously influenced by our bodies, our minds, and the various social environments in which we find ourselves. Not surprisingly, then, many of the problems that people face do not fall naturally into categories of "mental" or "physical" health. Violence is a good example, as are divorce and financial crises (such as the one the world experienced beginning in the first decade of the new millennium). Are these biological events? Psychological? Social? The answer is all of the above, including all of their complex interactions.

Violent crime, divorce, economic downturns, and social issues such as racism and sexism clearly affect human beings, but they are not in and of themselves "psychological" events. Nonetheless, they have two very important things in common that help us to understand how they are intimately linked to the invisibility of men's vulnerability.

First, they are important social experiences that affect *many people at once.* In other words, these are collective experiences whose effects cannot be reduced to individual people. Children, for example, are affected by divorce, and marriages are affected by children. Racism and sexism affect everyone because they limit human potential through repression and discrimination. Economic depressions can create significant mental health problems for those most affected, and the mental health of individuals in turn affects their productivity, which has direct effects on the economic conditions of societies. All of these examples show how individuals, communities, and global societies are linked through important social processes that affect us all.

The second point is that the effects of these events, on a grand scale, also depend on how humans react to them. Imagine the different effects of unemployment during a worldwide financial crisis depending on whether you are a wealthy person with a large extended family close by, or you are a poor recent immigrant with little to no social support.

Now imagine the different consequences of keeping quiet versus talking about social health problems involving men. Consider the example of school shootings. My colleague and friend Chris Kilmartin has repeatedly pointed out two important facts about school violence. First, the overwhelming majority of so-called school violence is actually committed by boys and men. Second, the fact that this is true (i.e., it is clearly a gendered problem in society) is rarely if ever mentioned. Instead, it is taken as normal, even acceptable, that young boys will periodically be violent to the point of mass murder. Failing to label the problem as a problem of boys and men keeps that part of it hidden from view and makes it that much more difficult to solve; if as a society we are not seeing that something about being a young boy is linked to these violent acts, we are not in a position to do much about them.

If you dig a little deeper into the issues surrounding young men and violence, you quickly see silence and invisibility playing additional roles. While not every lonely and ostracized adolescent boy goes on a shooting rampage, a recent review of fifteen school shootings between 1991 and 2005 found that, in addition to all the shooters being male, in thirteen out of the fifteen cases, these boys faced significant and repeated bullying or other forms of social rejection.[1] It seems safe to assume that their inner struggles played at least a partial role in setting into motion the tragedies that ensued. The practice of remaining silent when young boys or adolescents face significant emotional or social challenges in life can have devastating effects when these boys have nowhere else to turn and no healthy way to express their struggles.[2]

School shootings are an example of a *social health problem*. Social health involves the well-being of humans as social systems, not only as individuals—although the two are intimately linked, of course. Social health occurs at a number of levels, from our global society down to our local neighborhoods. Social health is important because it is something that we all share as part of our increasingly interconnected world. An excessively violent society, for example, is not healthy. Neighborhoods that do not have sufficient economic resources are not healthy neighborhoods, and so on.

Other examples abound if we open our eyes. Drug and alcohol abuse affects the social health of communities, and they are far more common in men than in women. One of the purposes of abusing drugs and alcohol is to numb or otherwise escape from painful emotions. Thus our tendency to encourage men to avoid their vulnerabilities may well be contributing to the epidemics of drug and alcohol abuse we see in numerous countries.

The way Americans do (or do not) support returning troops from Iraq and Afghanistan is another example of the way silence and invisibility affect the collective social health of the United States. Suicide rates among returning veterans are rising, as are rates of undiagnosed and untreated post-traumatic stress disorder, depression, and other psychiatric problems.[3] When we turn a blind eye or a deaf ear to the suffering of returning veterans, who are mostly men, significant social health problems result. These include unemployment, divorce, substance abuse, and crime. The bottom line is that silence and invisibility affect not only individual men and their families but also neighborhoods, communities, and societies in general.

## DO THINGS CHANGE? PROGRESS AND REGRESS

One of the most common questions writers and reporters like to ask is whether gender roles have changed since the baby boomers were born following World War II. The question is understandable. In many ways this is an ideal time for men to make major changes in the way they approach problems and challenges in their lives. It seems possible, perhaps now more than ever, to do what my colleague Ron Levant refers to as *reconstructing masculinity*, defining new meanings for manhood that are healthier, both physically and mentally.[4] At the same time, traditional notions of hypermasculinity are alive and well and more than ready to contest societal changes that are perceived to run the risk of overly feminizing men. The popularity of Ultimate Fighting, the continued presence of homophobic hate crimes, and the wide variety of misogynistic and antifeminist discourse in the public domain are but a few examples.

It is tempting to conclude that the more things change the more they stay the same, but that simply begs the question of why such patterns exist. A more dynamic perspective would emphasize the ways in which progress and regress are constantly in flux at a societal level. Depending on your perspective, the same events can often be interpreted either as signs of positive change or as more evidence of the status quo. Potential evidence comes in a variety of forms. Statistical trends are one type of indicator. As one example, there are now more stay-at-home and single fathers in the United States than ever before in recorded history.[5] Popular media trends are another source of evidence that traditional gender roles may be changing. Who would have predicted twenty years ago that a psychotherapy-seeking mob boss could become such a compelling character on mainstream television in the United States?

Finally, certain events have the potential to catalyze change through rapid mass media coverage. Two recent ones in the high-visibility, big-money world of professional sports illustrate particularly well the power of silence and invisibility in men's lives, the potential for change, and the social forces that resist it. In both cases a man's life was altered dramatically and irreversibly within twenty-four hours. In both cases their lives were inextricably linked to societal processes that had a dramatic effect on how their personal pain was viewed on a grand scale. The first case underscores the vast distance we still have to travel in order to render men's vulnerability more visible and audible at a societal level. The second case shows just how quickly and easily these changes can occur if you are paying attention and able to see gender operating within them.

## CAN A TIGER BE A VICTIM?

In November 2009 the undisputed world's best professional golfer, Tiger Woods, saw his world shattered. The details that made their way into the public sphere were remarkably consistent. Within twenty-four hours virtually anyone in the world had access to the following information:

- Tiger Woods was discovered by the police near his house, apparently having crashed his car into a fire hydrant at a slow speed.
- His face was badly injured.
- His wife was standing next to the car with a golf club.
- The car windshield was shattered.
- The driver's-side airbag had not deployed.

The police on the scene reported that Tiger's wife said she discovered the accident when she ran after him following an argument. She reported that she found Tiger trapped, so she ran back home to get a golf club to smash the window and rescue him. Several months later it was reported that when paramedics arrived on the scene they did not let Tiger's wife ride in the ambulance because they suspected a case of domestic violence.

Let me be 100 percent clear: I have no idea what actually happened in this incident, and I am not concerned with determining what did, or speculating about it. On the other hand, the various media reactions to the events have the potential to shed quite a bit of light on which aspects of masculinity and vulnerability we are prepared and not prepared to see in our most cherished male celebrities.

The most striking aspect of silence and invisibility in Tiger's story was the media's and the public's reaction to the possibility that he had been physically attacked by his wife, or the suggestion that he be considered a victim of intimate partner violence. Both private and public silence played a crucial role; Tiger was adamant that nothing of the sort occurred and the exact details were swept under the rug as quickly as possible, to be replaced by numerous reports of Tiger's infidelities.

On the public front, the possibility that Tiger was abused by his wife was met with one-liners, comedic YouTube videos, and *Saturday Night Live* skits. In the days that followed the initial events, the dominant messages were remarkably clear and consistent: if Tiger Woods was in fact physically abused by his wife, (a) it was funny rather than serious, and (b) he deserved it. One widely circulated video, for example, showed a tiger mascot at a baseball game being chased by a cheerleader with a massive golf club. A huge crowd is visible in the background laughing uproariously.

There may be readers who have a hard time understanding why I am troubled by these events. After all, Tiger had numerous affairs with other women and his wife was apparently unaware of this throughout their marriage. Plus society has long "known" that men are the major perpetrators of domestic violence. This information might lead a person to conclude both that Tiger had it coming and that the abuse couldn't have been very serious if the victim was a man. Neither of these perspectives, from my point of view, suggests that we have made much progress in acknowledging the realities of men's silent and invisible pain. To begin with, violence between intimate partners is never justified

unless someone fears for their life. Moreover, although historically it is clear that men have perpetrated far more violence against
women than the reverse, there is increasing evidence that the
number of men who are victims of violence at the hands of their
female partners is on the rise.[6]

My point is not that we should move from viewing domestic
violence as a women's problem to viewing it as a men's problem. It
is a problem for everyone and one that should not be mocked
or ridiculed. What concerns me is our societal unwillingness to
seriously entertain the possibility that a man as powerful, as
widely respected, and as influential as Tiger Woods could in fact
be a victim of violence at the hands of his wife. Based on what
emerged on the Internet, television, and radio after Tiger's story
broke, I am hard-pressed to see this as a sign of progress.

## THE WRONG CALL

Whereas Tiger's story illustrates our reluctance to acknowledge
vulnerability among our most celebrated men, another recent sporting event illustrates the potential payoffs of doing so. On June 2,
2010, Detroit Tigers' pitcher Armando Galarraga was one out away
from pitching a perfect baseball game; no runs, no hits, no walks,
no opposing players ever reaching first base. A perfect game is an
extremely rare event in baseball. The first such game was pitched in
1880, and only twenty have been recorded since that time.

With two outs in the top of the ninth inning, Cleveland Indi-
ans' batter Jim Donald hit a routine ground ball to the Tigers' first
baseman, Miguel Cabrera. The pitcher, Galarraga, covered first base,
and when Cabrera made the throw the crowd erupted in applause
for Galarraga's successful completion of a perfect game. There was
only one problem. First-base umpire Jim Joyce called Donald safe,

and in doing so turned Galarraga's historic accomplishment into a routine win for the Tigers. The crowd was stunned, as were sportscasters, media analysts, and baseball fans around the world. The instant replay was indisputable; Donald was clearly out by a good three feet, and Galarraga had indeed thrown a perfect game. Umpire Joyce had botched the call and deprived Galarraga, the Tigers, and all fans of baseball of what was rightly theirs.

Blown calls by umpires are nothing new in baseball. And when the calls really matter, as this one did, a single error in judgment can turn an umpire's life upside down in a matter of seconds. In game six of the 1985 World Series, the umpire Don Denkinger blew a call that may well have cost the St. Louis Cardinals the championship. At the time, Denkinger did not concede that he made a mistake. In the aftermath he was crucified in the press. Some disk jockeys in St. Louis even broadcast Denkinger's home address and phone number. Denkinger received a large amount of hate mail and even death threats.

In 2010, Jim Joyce responded to his own mistake in a very different way, and the series of events that followed were entirely unlike those that came in the wake of Denkinger's error. First, Joyce admitted that he blew the call and never once attempted to justify or excuse his mistake. In subsequent interviews Joyce was near tears at points as he repeated the phrases "I kicked the shit out of it. I missed it. Nobody feels worse than me." An article in the *Detroit Free Press* on June 8 reported the following:

> On the way to Comerica Park on Thursday, Joyce wondered whether he would be able to keep umping. He hadn't slept. He hadn't eaten. And although the night before hadn't unfolded with near the ugliness he feared, he still expected hostility when he walked onto the field early in the afternoon.

To his disbelief, many in the crowd rose and applauded. Then Galarraga met him at the plate with the lineup card. He teared up. Then first baseman Miguel Cabrera, who had lit into him right after the play, strolled past and patted him with his glove as he took the field to begin the game. Afterward, Joyce stood in the tunnel and choked back more tears.

In the weeks that followed, Joyce was voted one of the best umpires in baseball. He and Galarraga also appeared together on television to present an ESPY award for the most memorable moment in sports. Joyce was widely praised for his honesty and directness, and his willingness to take responsibility for his mistake. What struck me most about Joyce's story was how clearly he revealed his own vulnerability and the rewards he received for doing so. An umpire's job is to remain largely *invisible* during and after a game. Yet Joyce chose to let himself be seen. All of his uncertainty, self-criticism, shame, and embarrassment were widely available for public consumption. And rather than being further vilified for it, Joyce received compassion, support, and respect. I believe there is a lesson to be learned from Joyce's experience that applies to all men: the expression of honest vulnerability can sometimes pay huge dividends. Stories like Joyce's suggest that society may be increasingly willing to acknowledge silent and invisible pain in men. If that is true, there are several concrete steps that we can take to capitalize on the momentum.

## SOCIETAL CHANGE

Several years ago the phrase "think globally, act locally" came into fashion in the United States. It makes sense. There are significant global challenges facing all of us, and there are small changes that we can make in our day-to-day lives that can help overcome them. Of course, the opposite is also true: "think locally, act globally." When it comes to human well-being, many of the factors that most strongly affect it occur in our daily lives. Thus, when I look at potential ways to enhance men's physical, social, and emotional well-being, I see a clear need for changes that directly impact men's, women's, and children's lives. I will consider three examples of societal-level changes that have the potential to remove the shroud of silence and invisibility surrounding men's lives.

## PUBLIC POLICY

There are numerous opportunities to develop social policies that aid in recognizing hidden distress in men. For example, our approach to the provision of mental health services in the United States seems to have been driven by the assumption that "if you build it, they will come." Yet it is patently obvious that the majority of men who may benefit from consulting with a professional never get that far. As I mentioned in the previous chapter, a major part of the problem is the fact that mental health services are typically not designed with traditional masculinity in mind. As a result, we consider it typical for men not to seek help from a primary care physician or counselor because "guys don't do that." This notion serves to reinforce men's maladaptive responses to emotional distress and perpetuates the problem. What is needed are local and national policies that promote alternative points of view ("men *do* have difficulties, and men *do* seek help").

Research has shown that the way potential sources of help are packaged and presented has a strong impact on their acceptability to people who might consider using them.[7] In our own research program, we have found that more traditional men often are resistant to stereotypical presentations of "therapy." At the same time, these men express a strong interest in discussing their struggles with others and sharing what they have learned about how to cope with the stresses of living. There is a clear need to develop nontraditional forms of helping services that avoid the stigma associated with what we currently conceive of as "mental health care."

For example, in Australia, the Men's Shed movement gathers groups of men to rebuild abandoned buildings that then serve as support centers for the men to share their lives with each other. In the United States, the National Institutes of Health recently developed the "Real Men Real Depression" public awareness campaign. This online and print resource presents stories about real men from diverse backgrounds who have battled depression in their lives.

## BOYS TO MEN

There is a clear need for policies aimed at emotional education for boys. The practice of remaining silent when young boys or adolescents face significant emotional or social challenges in life can have devastating effects when they have nowhere else to turn and no healthy ways to express their struggles. Much of the process of gendered social learning I described in part 1 takes place among peers, and school is a major context where it unfolds. Given our current national emphasis on academic achievement and standardized testing, while simultaneously decreasing funding for public schools, we are in danger of ignoring the importance of social and emotional development among children and adolescents.

When considering what sorts of policies and practices to institute with young boys and men, we must resist the temptation to be swayed by overly simple solutions based on highly polarized generalizations about the differences between boys and girls. The polarizing lenses I described in chapter 5 affect not only individuals in society but also government officials, policy makers, and organizations that develop and disseminate new social policies. For example, there is currently a movement in the United States to segregate boys and girls during elementary and secondary schooling. It gains considerable momentum from the apparently scientific findings that boys' and girls' brains are wired differently, and thus they must learn differently as well. This is a highly controversial set of issues. For the present purposes, simply note that the notion that boys' and girls' brains are "wired differently" is far from conclusive. In fact, the bulk of scientific data on brain development indicates far more similarities than differences between the sexes. Moreover, if there are in fact important biological differences in learning styles between boys and girls, this does not necessarily justify separating them.

## TALKING ABOUT (TALKING ABOUT) GENDER

Perhaps the biggest potential payoff will come from changing the way we talk about gender in our day-to-day lives. This is not a matter of talking *more* about gender; between the polarizing lenses, popular books, television shows, et cetera, we already consume more than our fair share of beliefs, assumptions, and ideologies about "the differences between women and men." But what is sorely lacking in contemporary society is greater individual awareness of *how talking about gender operates.* In other words, while we are quite comfortable talking about gender, we rarely if ever talk *about* talking about gender.

Put another way, we spend a lot of time talking about what we think is true, whether it be our own opinions, scientific findings, or other claims about the nature of men and women. Yet we rarely, if ever, consider how helpful or harmful it is to talk about issues in different ways. We proceed instead as if our own statements and ideas are transparent representations of reality with no underlying agendas or attitudes; after all, we are simply "reporting the facts." In contrast, those who study the way human beings use language to represent reality have concluded that nothing could be farther from the truth.

Theorizing about our own and other people's behavior is a part of everyday life. Human beings are natural reason-givers. We are always attempting to account for our own and others' actions. Why is my child spending more time with friends than with family? Why did my boss make critical comments about my colleague's work? Why do people vote Democrat or Republican? Why am I tired today? Why don't men discuss their feelings? The list goes on.

We rarely, if ever, offer answers to these questions from some sort of neutral, scientific, or objective point of view. In fact, it is nearly impossible to do this because different theories have different consequences for how we feel about an issue. Different theories also point to different potential actions, and they suggest different ways to attribute blame for problems. The bottom line is that as individuals we are invested in how we and others view different theories of human behavior.

To get a sense of this, just remember the last time you discussed issues such as poverty, politics, terrorism, or mental illness with people whose point of view was different from yours. How quickly did an otherwise rational conversation turn heated? The same holds true for conversations about men and why they are the way they are. When we ask, "Why are men's inner lives so invisible in modern society?" we can't help but also implicitly ask the following questions:

1. How should we feel about the fact that so much silence surrounds men's well-being?
2. Is it a problem or not?
3. If so, whose fault is it?
4. Can we do anything about it?
5. If so, what should we do?

We may not be talking about these issues directly, but they're running right alongside the conversation and providing much of the emotional energy. This means that the nature of men's well-being is not an easy thing to figure out. There's too much emotion surrounding it. As a result, we find ourselves quickly falling into highly polarized and oversimplified debates ("It is all in the genes," "It's society's fault for teaching men to be this way," and so on). Understanding your own motivation for liking or disliking different theories can help you to develop a broader and more objective understanding of what is going on when men keep silent or invisible.

The accompanying table summarizes three common lay theories about men's tendency to keep their vulnerabilities hidden. The first column presents the guts of the theory in simplified form. The next four columns present what I call *moral riders*. These moral riders are often along for the ride when we engage in regular theorizing about important social issues such as men's silence and invisibility. They have implications for how we should feel about men's silence, what we might do about it (or not do about it), and who is to blame for any problems. What I mean by *along for the ride* is that these moral riders are potentially powerful influences on the outcome of whatever we are talking about, *even though we are not talking about them directly*. They are the underlying moral questions that we are often implicitly debating with one another, or with ourselves, while we try on the surface to be objective

| THEORY | MORAL RIDERS | | | |
|---|---|---|---|---|
| This Theory | Means . . . | So We Should . . . | And We Might Feel . . . | Whose Fault Is It? |
| Men are just this way | It is not worth talking about | Do nothing | Acceptance, resignation, anger | Men |
| Men are taught to be this way | It is all how you were raised | Change how we raise boys / treat men | Empathy, compassion | Parents / Society |
| Men are hardwired to be this way | It is all in the genes, there's no way around it | Better accommodate men's natural tendencies | Compassion, indifference, resignation | Nobody? Evolution? |

reporters of our ideas. Becoming aware of their presence can empower you to develop a more objective perspective on how silence and invisibility actually operate. The goal is to become able to view men's behavior as a social scientist would, rather than as a person directly involved in the situation with all of the emotional baggage that entails. You can always step back into it, so to speak. But being able to step out of it and see it clearly for what it is, without the moral riders, will be tremendously helpful to you.

## THE POLITICAL LANDSCAPE OF MEN'S INNER LIVES

As you gain more insight into the psychology of men, you may find yourself discussing it with other people. In this case, it is helpful to know the political landscape. There is a great deal of variation in the way different groups of people think about the problems facing men. Nonetheless, for the sake of gaining some familiarity with the political landscape, here are some of the more well-established political perspectives on men.

*Men's rights.* These individuals believe that men are being treated unfairly in many domains of life. They are often hostile toward feminism and believe that much of the progress women have made has come at the expense of men. Not surprisingly, they often see negative effects on men's well-being coming from unfair treatment of men. If asked why men's inner lives are so silent, someone coming from a men's rights perspective might say, "Why should we speak up about what we feel? We'll only be shot down." If asked how we can better men's well-being, the answer is usually that we need to do a better job advocating for men.

*Men's inner essence.* These individuals believe that the true inner essence of being a man has been lost in this modern overly feminized world. They can be sympathetic to theories suggesting that the deep roots of men's minds lie in their evolutionary past as hunter-gatherers. If asked how we can better men's well-being, the answer is usually that we need to do a better job creating meaningful connections between men, particularly in father-son relationships where young boys are taught what it means to be a man.

*Men's liberation.* These individuals believe that, just as women have been historically oppressed by stereotypical rules for femininity, men have been harmed by the restrictive nature of masculine gender roles. They believe in enhancing men's well-being (and by extension, the well-being of women, children, and communities) by challenging these traditional roles and creating new meanings of manhood that are ultimately more adaptive. If asked why men tend to keep their emotional pain hidden from others, these individuals would suggest that the true causes lie in the messages men receive from society about what it means to be a man.

As you may imagine, each of these political perspectives has numerous moral riders that drive particular beliefs, ideologies, and attitudes. When you engage in a conversation with others about the psychology of men, these political perspectives and their accompanying moral riders often play a significant role in how the conversation unfolds. By recognizing them for what they are, you can begin to extricate yourself from unproductive, highly polarized debates that typically serve to further reinforce political divides rather than promoting greater understanding of and compassion for both men and women. Part of the challenge is that each of these perspectives claims to have cornered the market on the causes of men's behavior. And in doing so, they obscure the useful contributions that other perspectives may have to offer.

## SUMMARY

The silence and invisibility that surround men's emotional lives are not only psychological in nature but also social and historical. Staying hidden is an individual choice, but the causes and consequences of hidden pain extend far beyond individual men. This means that to successfully address the problem requires seeing beyond individual psychology.

Social health, in contrast, involves the well-being of humans as social systems, from local neighborhoods all the way up to our increasingly global society. Several steps are required to remedy the problems caused by men's silence at a societal level. The first is developing public policies that establish and reinforce men's well-being as a major social concern for all human beings. The second is recognizing the needs of young boys and men who are systematically discouraged from taking their inner lives seriously and sharing them with others. Finally, it benefits us all to become more aware of the political landscapes that surround men's vulnerability.

Different theories as to why men are often silent and invisible carry with them different implicit assumptions about what the problems are, how they should be addressed, and how we should feel about them. Rather than being simply neutral, objective, or scientific theories, they often contain moral agendas that have a strong influence on how we feel toward men.

# REFERENCES

## 1: INVISIBLE MEN . . . WHO ARE YOU KIDDING?!

1. O'Neil, J. M. 2008. Summarizing 25 years of research on men's gender role conflict using the Gender Role Conflict Scale: New research paradigms and clinical implications. *Counseling Psychologist* 36:358–445.

2. Whorley, M., and Addis, M. E. 2006. Ten years of research on the psychology of men and masculinity in the United States: Methodological trends and critique. *Sex Roles* 55:649–58.

3. Addis, M. E. 2008. Gender and depression in men. *Clinical Psychology: Science and Practice* 15:153–68.

4. Kaplan, M. S., Huguet, N., McFarland, B. H., and Newsom, J. T. 2007. Suicide among male veterans: A prospective population-based study. *Journal of Epidemiology and Community Health* 61: 619–24.

5. Kuehn, B. M. 2009. Soldier suicide rates continue to rise: Military, scientists work to stem the tide. *Journal of the American Medical Association* 301 (11): 1111–13.

6. Levant, R. F., Good, G. E., Cook, Stephen W., O'Neil, J. M., Smalley, K. B., Owen, K., and Richmond, K. 2006. The normative Male

Alexithymia Scale: Measurement of a gender-linked syndrome. *Psychology of Men and Masculinity* 7 (4): 212–24.

7. Bagby, M. R., Taylor, G. J., and Parker, J. D. A. 1994. The twenty-item Toronto Alexithymia scale—II. Convergent, discriminant, and concurrent validity. *Journal of Psychosomatic Research* 38 (1): 33–40.

8. Levant, R. F., and Kopecky, G. 1995. *Masculinity reconstructed: Changing the rules of manhood—at work, in relationships, and in family life.* New York: Dutton.

9. Dindia, K., and Allen, M. 1992. Sex differences in self-disclosure: A meta-analysis. *Psychological Bulletin* 112 (1): 106–24.

10. Shaffer, D. R., Pegalis, L. J., and Cornell, D. P. 1992. Gender and self-disclosure revisited: Personal and contextual variations in self-disclosure to same-sex acquaintances. *Journal of Social Psychology* 132 (3): 307–15.

11. Foubert, J. D., and Sholley, B. K. 1996. Effects of gender, gender role, and individualized trust on self-disclosure. *Handbook of Gender Research* 11 (5): 277–88.

12. Brown, L. M., Lamb, S., and Tappan, M. 2009. *Packaging boyhood: Saving our sons from superheroes, slackers, and other media stereotypes.* New York: St. Martin's Press.

## 2: THE CAUSES OF SILENCE AND INVISIBILITY

1. Buck, R. 1977. Non-verbal communication of affect in preschool children: Relationships with personality and skin conductance. *Journal of Personality and Social Psychology* 35 (4):225–36.

2. Brody, L. 1985. Gender differences in emotional development: A review of theories and research. *Journal of Personality* 53:14–59.

3. Stapley, J. C., and Haviland, J. M. 1989. Beyond depression: Gender differences in normal adolescents' emotional experiences. *Sex Roles* 20:295–308.

4. Malatesta, C. Z., and Haviland, J. M. 1982. Learning display

rules: The socialization of emotion expression in infancy. *Child Development* 53 (4): 991–1003.

5. Barkow, J. H., Cosmides, L., and Tooby, J., eds. 1992. *The adapted mind: Evolutionary psychology and the generation of culture.* Oxford and New York: Oxford University Press.

6. Miller, G. 2001. *The mating mind: How sexual choice shaped the evolution of human nature.* New York: Anchor.

7. Levant, R. F., and Pollack, W. S., eds. 1995. *A new psychology of men.* New York: Basic Books.

8. Kilmartin, C. 2009. *The masculine self.* 4th ed. New York: Sloan.

9. Miller, G. 2001. *The mating mind: How sexual choice shaped the evolution of human nature.* New York: Anchor.

10. Mahalik, J. R., Locke, B. D., Ludlow, L. H., Diemer, M. A., Scott, R. P. J., Gottfried, M., and Freitas, G. 2003. Development of the conformity to masculine norms inventory. *Psychology of Men and Masculinity* 4 (1): 3–25.

11. Mahalik, J., Morray, E., Coonerty-Femiano, A., Ludlow, L., Slattery, S., and Smiler, A. 2005. Development of the conformity to feminine norms inventory. *Sex Roles* 52 (7–8): 417–35.

12. Chaplin, T. M., Cole, P. M., and Zahn-Wexler, C. 2005. Parental socialization of emotion expression: Gender differences and relations to child adjustment. *Emotion* 5:80–88.

13. Eisenberg, N., Cumberland, A., and Spinrad, T. L. 1998. Parental socialization of emotion. *Psychological Inquiry* 9:241–73.

14. Wichstrom, L. 1999. The emergence of gender difference in depressed mood during adolescence: The role of intensified gender socialization. *Developmental Psychology* 35:232–45.

15. Broderick, P. C. 1998. Early adolescent gender differences in the use of ruminative and distracting coping strategies. *Journal of Early Adolescence* 18:173–91.

16. Sethi, S., and Nolen-Hoeksema, S. 1997. Gender differences in internal and external focusing among adolescents. *Sex Roles* 37:687–700.

17. Chaplin, T. M., Cole, P. M., and Zahn-Wexler, C. 2005. Parental socialization of emotion expression: Gender differences and relations to child adjustment. *Emotion* 5:80–88.

18. Kring, A. M., and Bachorowski, J. 1999. Emotions and psychopathology. *Cognition and Emotion* 13:575–99.

19. Eisenberg, N., Cumberland, A., and Spinrad, T. L. 1998. Parental socialization of emotion. *Psychological Inquiry* 9:241–73.

## 3: SILENCE AND INVISIBILITY IN YOUR LIFE

1. Cho, H. 2007. Influences of self-monitoring and goal-setting on drinking refusal self-efficacy and drinking behavior. *Alcoholism Treatment Quarterly* 25 (3): 53–65.

2. Craske, M. G., and Tsao, J. C. I. 1999. Self-monitoring with panic and anxiety disorders. *Psychological Assessment* 11 (4): 466–79.

3. Harmon, T. M., Nelson, R. O., and Hayes, S. C. 1980. Self-monitoring of mood versus activity by depressed clients. *Journal of Consulting and Clinical Psychology* 48 (1): 30–38.

4. Levant, R. F., Good, G. E., Cook, S. W., O'Neil, J. M., Smalley, K. B., Owen, K., and Richmond, K. 2006. The normative Male Alexithymia Scale: Measurement of a gender-linked syndrome. *Psychology of Men and Masculinity* 7 (4): 212–24.

5. O'Neil, J. M. 2008. Summarizing 25 years of research on men's gender role conflict using the Gender Role Conflict Scale: New research paradigms and clinical implications. *Counseling Psychologist* 36:358–445.

6. Whorley, M., and Addis, M. E. 2006. Ten years of research on the psychology of men and masculinity in the United States: Methodological trends and critique. *Sex Roles* 55:649–58.

7. Mahalik, J. R., Locke, B. D., Ludlow, L. H., Diemer, M. A., Scott, R. P. J., Gottfried, M., and Freitas, G. 2003. Development of the conformity to masculine norms inventory. *Psychology of Men and Masculinity* 4 (1): 3–25.

8. Addis, M. E., and Mahalik, J. R. 2003. Men, masculinity, and the contexts of help seeking. *American Psychologist* 58:5–14.

9. O'Neil, J. M. 2008. Summarizing 25 years of research on men's gender role conflict using the Gender Role Conflict Scale: New research paradigms and clinical implications. *Counseling Psychologist* 36:358–445.

10. Graef, S. T., Tokar, D. M., and Kaut, K. P. 2010. Relations of masculinity ideology, conformity to masculine role norms, and masculine gender role conflict to men's attitudes toward and willingness to seek career counseling. *Psychology of Men and Masculinity* 11 (4): 319–33.

11. Good, G. E., and Wood, P. K. 1995. Male gender role conflict, depression, and help seeking: Do college men face double jeopardy? *Journal of Counseling and Development* 74:70–75.

## 4: PHYSICAL WELL-BEING

1. Barry, D. 1995. *Dave Barry's complete guide to guys.* New York: Ballantine Books.

2. Courtenay, W. H. 2000. Constructions of masculinity and their influence on men's well-being: A theory of gender and health. *Social Science and Medicine* 50:1385–401.

3. Bertakis, K. D., Helms, L. J., Callahan, E. J., Azari, R., Leigh, P., and Robbins, J. A. 2001. Patient gender differences in the diagnosis of depression in primary care. *Journal of Women's Health and Gender-Based Medicine* 10:689–98.

4. Potts, M. K., Burnam, M. A., and Wells, K. B. 1991. Gender differences in depression detection: A comparison of clinician diagnosis and standardized assessment. *Psychological Assessment* 3:609–15.

5. Simon, G. E., and Von Korff, M. 1995. Recognition, management, and outcomes of depression in primary care. *Archives of Family Medicine* 4:99–105.

6. Windle, C. R., and Smith, D. A. 2009. Withdrawal moderates the association between husband gender role conflict and wife marital adjustment. *Psychology of Men and Masculinity* 10 (4): 245–60.

7. Rochlen, A. B., and Mahalik, J. R. 2004. Women's perceptions of male partners' gender role conflict as predictors of psychological well-being and relationship satisfaction. *Psychology of Men and Masculinity* 5 (2): 147–57.

8. Mondaini, N., Ponchietti, R., Gontero, P., Muir, G. H., Natali, A., Di Loro, F., Caldarera, E., Biscioni, S., and Rizzo, M. 2002. Penile length is normal in most men seeking penile lengthening procedures. *International Journal of Impotence Research* 14:283–86.

9. Lever, J., Frederick, D. A., and Peplau, L. A. 2006. Does size matter? Men's and women's views on penis size across the lifespan. *Psychology of Men and Masculinity* 7 (3): 129–43.

## 5: EMOTIONAL WELL-BEING

1. Kessler, R. C. 1997. The effects of stressful life events on depression. *Annual Review of Psychology* 48:191–214.

2. Leserman, J., Petitto, J. M., Golden, R. N., Gaynes, B. N., Gu, H., Perkins, D. O., Silva, S. G., Folds, J. D., and Evans, D. L. 2000. Impact of stressful life events, depression, social support, coping, and cortisol on progression to AIDS. *American Journal of Psychiatry* 157 (8): 1221–28.

3. Seidlitz, L., Wyer, R. S., and Diener, E. 1997. Cognitive correlates of subjective well-being: The processing of valenced life events by happy and unhappy persons. *Journal of Research in Personality* 31 (2): 240–56.

4. Diener, E. 2009. Subjective well-being. The science of well being: The collected works of Ed Diener. *Social Indicators Research Series* 37:11–58.

5. Hyde, J. S. 2005. The gender similarities hypothesis. *American Psychologist* 60 (6): 581–92.

6. Fisher, A. H., ed. 2000. *Gender and emotion: Social psychological perspectives*. New York: Cambridge University Press.

7. Jacobson, N. S., and Truax, P. 1991. Clinical significance: A statistical approach to defining meaningful change in psychotherapy research. *Journal of Consulting and Clinical Psychology* 59 (1): 12–19.

8. Bem, S. L. 1993. *The lenses of gender: Transforming the debate on sexual inequality.* New Haven, Conn.: Yale University Press.

9. Gladwell, M. 2005. *Blink: The power of thinking without thinking.* New York: Little, Brown.

10. Dooley, D., and Catalano, R. 1988. Recent research on psychological effects of unemployment. *Journal of Social Issues* 44 (4): 1–12.

11. Price, R. H., Choi, J. N., and Vinokur, A. D. 2002. Links in the chain of adversity following job loss: How financial strain and loss of personal control lead to depression, impaired functioning, and poor health. *Journal of Occupational Health Psychology* 7 (4): 302–12.

12. Gotlib, I. H., and Hammen, C. L., eds. 2002. *Handbook of depression.* New York: Guilford Press.

13. Addis, M. E. 2008. Gender and depression in men. *Clinical Psychology: Science and Practice* 15:153–68.

14. Addis, M. E., Hatgis, C., Krasnow, A. D., Jacob, K., Bourne, L., and Mansfield, A. 2004. Effectiveness of cognitive-behavioral treatment for panic disorder versus treatment as usual in a managed care setting. *Journal of Consulting and Clinical Psychology* 72 (4): 625–35.

15. Addis, M. E., Hatgis, C., Cardemil, E., Jacob, K., Krasnow, A. D., and Mansfield, A. 2006. Effectiveness of cognitive-behavioral treatment for panic disorder versus treatment as usual in a managed care setting: 2-year follow-up. *Journal of Consulting and Clinical Psychology* 74 (2): 377–85.

16. Fennel, M. J. V., and Tensdale, J. D. 1987. Cognitive therapy for depression: Individual differences and the process of change. *Cognitive Therapy and Research* 11:253–72.

17. Gilmore, D. D. 1991. *Manhood in the making: Cultural concepts of masculinity.* New Haven, Conn.: Yale University Press.

18. Addis, M. E., and Mahalik, J. R. 2003. Men, masculinity, and the contexts of help seeking. *American Psychologist* 58:5–14.

19. Pennebaker, J. W., Kiecolt-Glaser, J. K., and Glaser, R. 1988. Disclosure of traumas and immune function: Health implications for psychotherapy. *Journal of Consulting and Clinical Psychology* 56 (2): 239–45.

20. Gross, J. J., and Levenson, R. W. 1993. Emotional suppression: Physiology, self-report, and expressive behavior. *Journal of Personality and Social Psychology* 64 (6): 970–86.

21. Wenzlaff, R. M., and Wegner, D. M. 2000. Thought suppression. *Annual Review of Psychology* 51:59–91.

## 6: RELATIONSHIP WELL-BEING

1. Smiler, A. P. 2008. "I wanted to get to know her better": Adolescent boys' dating motives, masculinity ideology, and sexual behavior. *Journal of Adolescence* 31 (1): 17–32.

2. Cordova, J. V., and Scott, R. L. 2001. Intimacy: A behavioral interpretation. *Behavior Analyst* 24 (1): 75–86.

3. Rotermann, M. 2007. Marital breakdown and subsequent depression. *Health Reports* 18:33–46.

4. Umberson, D., and Williams, C. L. 1993. Divorced fathers: Parental role strain and psychological distress. *Journal of Family Issues* 14 (3): 378–400.

5. Menaghan, E. G., and Lieberman, M. A. 1986. Changes in depression following divorce: A panel study. *Journal of Marriage and the Family* 48 (2): 319–28.

6. Aseltine, R. H., and Kessler, R. C. 1993. Marital disruption and depression in a community sample. *Journal of Health and Social Behavior* 34 (3): 237–51.

7. Christensen, A., and Jacobson, N. S. 2000. *Reconcilable differences*. New York: Guilford Press.

8. Pollack, W. 1998. *Real boys: Rescuing our sons from the myths of boyhood*. New York: Henry Holt.

9. Bergman, S. J. 1995. Men's psychological development: A relational perspective. In R. F. Levant and W. S. Pollack, eds., *A new psychology of men*, pp. 69–90. New York: Basic Books.

10. Eldridge, K. A., and Christensen, A. 2002. Demand-withdraw communication during couple conflict: A review and analysis. In P. Noller and J. A. Feeney, eds., *Understanding marriage: Developments in the study of couple interaction*, pp. 289–322. New York: Cambridge University Press.

11. Christensen, A., and Heavey, C. L. 1993. Gender differences in marital conflict: The demand/withdraw interaction pattern. In S. Oskamp and M. Costanzo, eds., *Gender issues in contemporary society*, pp. 113–41. Thousand Oaks, Calif.: Sage.

## 7: SILENCE AND INVISIBILITY IN MEN'S FRIENDSHIPS

1. Pollack, W. S. 1995. No man is an island: Toward a new psychoanalytic psychology of men. In R. F. Levant and W. S. Pollack, eds., *A new psychology of men*, pp. 33–67. New York: Basic Books.

2. Uchino, B. N., Cacioppo, J. T., and Kiecolt-Glaser, J. K. 1996. The relationship between social support and physiological processes: A review with emphasis on underlying mechanisms and implications for health. *Psychological Bulletin* 119:488–531.

3. Helgeson, V. S. 2003. Social support and quality of life. *Quality of Life Research* 12 (1): 25–31.

4. Wester, S. R., Christianson, H. F., Vogel, D. L., and Wei, M. 2007. Gender role conflict and psychological distress: The role of social support. *Psychology of Men and Masculinity* 8 (4): 215–24.

5. Swickert, R., and Hittner, J. 2009. Social support coping mediates the relationship between gender and posttraumatic growth. *Journal of Health Psychology* 14:387–93.

6. Nardi, P. 1992. *Men's friendships*. London: Sage.

7. Kimmel, M. S. 1994. Masculinity as homophobia: Fear, shame, and silence in the construction of gender identity. In H. Brod and M. Kaufman, eds., *Theorizing masculinities*, pp. 119–41. London: Sage.

8. Phoenix, A., Frosh, S., and Pattman, R. 2003. Producing contradictory masculine subject positions: Narratives of threat, homophobia, and bullying in 11–14 year old boys. *Journal of Social Issues* 59 (1): 179–95.

9. Sidman, M. 1989. *Coercion and its fallout*. Boston: Authors Cooperative.

10. Kimmel, M. S. 1994. Masculinity as homophobia: Fear, shame, and silence in the construction of gender identity. In H. Brod and M. Kaufman, eds., *Theorizing masculinities*, pp. 119–41. London: Sage.

## 8: COPING WITH STRESSFUL LIFE EVENTS

1. Center for Disease Control and National Center for Health Statistics.

2. Bruce, M. L., and Kim, K. M. 1992. Differences in the effects of divorce on major depression in men and women. *The American Journal of Psychiatry* 149 (7): 914–17.

3. Fine, M. A., and Harvey, J. H., eds. 2006. *Handbook of divorce and relationship dissolution*. Mahwah, N.J.: Lawrence Erlbaum.

4. Rotermann, M. 2007. Marital breakdown and subsequent depression. *Health Reports* 4 (18): 33–46.

5. Kposowa, A. J. 2000. Marital status and suicide in the National Longitudinal Mortality Study. *Journal of Epidemiology and Community Health* 54:254–61.

6. Dooley, D., and Catalano, R. 1988. Recent research on psychological effects of unemployment. *Journal of Social Issues* 44 (4): 1–12.

7. Price, R. H., Choi, J. N., and Vinokur, A. D. 2002. Links in the chain of adversity following job loss: How financial strain and loss

of personal control lead to depression, impaired functioning, and poor health. *Journal of Occupational Health Psychology* 7 (4): 302–12.

8. Addis, M. E., and Mahalik, J. R. 2003. Men, masculinity, and the contexts of help seeking. *American Psychologist* 58:5–14.

9. Van Boeijen, C. A., van Balkom, A. J. L. M., van Oppen, P., Blankenstein, N., Cherpanath, A., and van Dyck, R. 2005. Efficacy of self-help manuals for anxiety disorders in primary care: A systematic review. *Family Practice* 22 (2): 192–96.

10. Van der Houwen, K., Schut, H., van den Bout, J., Stroebe, M., and Stroebe, W. 2010. The efficacy of a brief internet-based self-help intervention for the bereaved. *Behaviour Research and Therapy* 48 (5): 359–67.

11. Dunn, A. L., Trivedi, M. H., Kampert, J. B., Clark, C. G., and Chambliss, H. O. 2005. Exercise treatment for depression: Efficacy and dose response. *American Journal of Preventive Medicine* 28 (1): 1–8.

## 9: SOCIETAL CHANGE

1. Leary, M. R., Kowalski, R. M., Smith, L., and Phillips, S. 2003. Teasing, rejection, and violence: Case studies of the school shootings. *Aggressive Behavior* 29 (3): 202–14.

2. Saval, M. 2009. *The secret lives of boys: Inside the raw emotional world of male teens.* New York: Basic Books.

3. Kaplan, M. S., Huguet, N., McFarland, B. H., and Newsom, J. T. 2007. Suicide among male veterans: A prospective population-based study. *Journal of Epidemiology and Community Health* 61:619–24.

4. Levant, R. F., and Kopecky, G. 1995. *Masculinity reconstructed: Changing the rules of manhood—at work, in relationships, and in family life.* New York: Dutton.

5. Rochlen, A. B., Suizzo, M. A., McKelley, R. A., and Scaringi, V. 2008. I'm just providing for my family: A qualitative study of stay-at-home fathers. *Psychology of Men and Masculinity* 9 (4): 193–206.

6. Hines, D. A., and Malley-Morrison, K. 2001. Psychological

effects of partner abuse against men: A neglected research area. *Psychology of Men and Masculinity* 2 (2):75–85.

7. Addis, M. E., and Carpenter, K. M. 1999. Why, why, why?: Reason-giving and rumination as predictors of response to activation and insight oriented treatment rationales. *Journal of Clinical Psychology* 55 (7): 881–94.

# ACKNOWLEDGMENTS

In February 2007, *Newsweek* magazine ran a cover story on the topic of men and depression. As part of the story a reporter visited our research group at Clark University in Worcester, Massachusetts. We spent a day talking about our work on developing new ways to talk to men about emotions, life problems, and other aspects of what has traditionally been considered "mental" health. I was pleased to see the work gathering some national attention, and even more pleased to see such a long-neglected topic front and center in the public eye.

At the same time, I was totally unprepared for the subsequent flood of phone calls from literary agents asking whether I was interested in writing a book on men and depression. First of all, I had no idea what a literary agent was. The prospect of referring to "my agent," were I to take on such a project, was sure to lead to more than a few sideways glances from friends and family. But more important, I found communicating with literary agents as a group to be difficult. A typical conversation went something like this:

LITERARY AGENT: This is really timely work, pretty amazing stuff. I think the world is ready for a book on men and depression, and I think you're the person to write it!

ME: Actually, there are already some very good books on that topic.

LITERARY AGENT: Oh. Really? Well, is there another book you've thought about writing?

ME: Yes. For the past couple of years I've been thinking about writing a book on silence and invisibility in men's lives. You see, I think there's a major problem in society that's been going on for some time having to do with—

LITERARY AGENT: No, not a broad enough appeal. How about silence and men's depression?

ME: Well, I see depression as one possible consequence of men's silence and invisibility, but the potential problems are far wider and greater. Let me explain. You see—

LITERARY AGENT: That's all right. I'm really more interested in a book on men and depression. All those veterans coming back from war, the economy, it's a hot topic.


I probably had ten such conversations in the span of two days, and I had just about vowed not to answer the phone for a week when I received a call from Lane Zachary at Zachary Schuster Harmsworth. Lane immediately struck me as a different type of literary agent, in the most positive sense, and she has remained so throughout our work together. Lane was far more interested in learning about my perspectives on men's well-being than she was in persuading me to write a particular kind of book. Over the last three years she has provided consistent guidance and support, and an invaluable education in the modern-day workings of the trade publishing business. I am convinced that I would never have gotten to the point of writing these acknowledgments without her involvement in the project. I could not have asked for a better agent.

My editor at Times Books, Serena Jones, has also been immensely helpful. I have been consistently impressed by her rapid grasp of the issues I've wrestled with in this book and her ability to provide concise and penetrating feedback. The end product is far better than it would have been without her involvement.

I also want to thank my many colleagues and friends in Division 51 of the American Psychological Association, the Society for the Psychological Study of Men and Masculinity. The pioneering members of this organization set the stage for generations of future work. Their courageous and creative forays into scholarship on the psychology of men have made this book possible. In particular, Gary Brooks, Chris Kilmartin, Jim Mahalik, Ron Levant, Jim O'Neil, Joseph Pleck, Aaron Rochlen, and Andrew Smiler have been instrumental in providing constructive criticism and support for many of the ideas in this book.

Over the last ten years I have been fortunate to work with an extremely talented group of graduate and undergraduate students at Clark University, including Josh Berger, Victoria Goldberg, Jon Green, Mariola Magovcevic, Abigail Mansfield, Andrew Ninnemann, Jen Primack, Chris Reigeluth, and Matt Syzdek. Their dedication to high-quality empirical research and conceptual rigor in their work has benefited my own work in countless ways. My colleagues and friends at Clark University, Esteban Cardemil, James Cordova, Wendy Grolnick, and Kelly Boulay, have also made going to work each day far less painful, and far more fun, that it would be otherwise. Clark University's motto is "Challenging Convention and Changing the World."

The community at Clark has given me the courage to try and do precisely that.

Special thanks go to my friends Barry Walsh, Harold Wingood, Paul Peterson, and Michael Gan. They are remarkable men, always there for support during difficult times, and always ready to celebrate when the sun shines.

My mother, Marsha Emmer Addis, has loved and supported me in the best way a parent can. Thank you for nurturing my hopes and dreams with the type of acceptance that has helped me to discover my own path. My father, Barnett Roy Addis, led by example in teaching me from a very young age that it is possible, and even preferable, to experience powerful emotions as a man and share them with others. He was never an invisible father, and for that I will always be grateful. Dina Lees, you are without a doubt the best FWWWIANROC a man could ever hope for. Thank you for your years of love and support, and for being the kind, compassionate, and supportive person that you continue to be. And finally, immeasurable gratitude goes to my daughter, Chloe Rachel Addis. You never cease to amaze me with your humor, grace, kindness, and intelligence. You make me proud to be, in your own words, "a feelings doctor." I am even more proud to be your father.

# INDEX

# ABOUT THE AUTHOR

MICHAEL E. ADDIS, PH.D., has published over seventy articles and books on a variety of topics related to treatments for depression and anxiety, the integration of science and clinical practice, and men's mental health. He is a past recipient of the American Psychological Association's David Shakow Award for early career contributions to the science and practice of clinical psychology and the New Researcher Award from the Association for Behavioral and Cognitive Therapies. He is a fellow of the American Psychological Association and past president of the Society for the Psychological Study of Men and Masculinity. Dr. Addis is currently a professor of psychology at Clark University in Worcester, Massachusetts. He lives in central Massachusetts.